DRAMA CLASSICS

The Drama Classics series aims to offer the world's greatest plays in affordable paperback editions for students, actors and theatregoers. The hallmarks of the series are accessible introductions, uncluttered texts and an overall theatrical perspective.

Given that readers may be encountering a particular play for the first time, the introduction seeks to fill in the theatrical/historical background and to outline the chief themes rather than concentrate on interpretational and textual analysis. Similarly the play-texts themselves are free of footnotes and other interpolations: instead there is an end-glossary of 'difficult' words and phrases.

The texts of the English-language plays in the series have been prepared taking full account of all existing scholarship. The foreign-language plays have been newly translated into a modern English that is both actable and accurate: many of the translators regularly have their work staged professionally.

Edited until his early death by Kenneth McLeish, the Drama Classics series continues with his aim of providing a first-class library of dramatic literature representing the best of world theatre.

Associate editors:
Professor Trevor R. Griffiths
Visiting Professor in Humanities, University of Hertfordshire
Dr Colin Counsell
*School of Humanities, Arts and Languages,
London Metropolitan University*

DRAMA CLASSICS *the first hundred*

The Alchemist
All for Love
Andromache
Antigone
Bacchae
Bartholomew Fair
The Beaux Stratagem
The Beggar's Opera
Birds
Blood Wedding
Celestina
The Changeling
A Chaste Maid in Cheapside
The Cherry Orchard
Children of the Sun
El Cid
The Country Wife
The Dance of Death
The Devil is an Ass
Doctor Faustus
A Doll's House
Don Juan
The Duchess of Malfi
Edward II
Electra (Euripides)
Electra (Sophocles)
An Enemy of the People
Everyman
Faust
A Flea in her Ear
Frogs
Fuente Ovejuna
The Game of Love and Chance
Ghosts
The Government Inspector
Hecuba
Hedda Gabler

The Hypochondriac
The Importance of Being Earnest
An Ideal Husband
An Italian Straw Hat
Ivanov
The Jew of Malta
The Knight of the Burning Pestle
The Lady from the Sea
The Learned Ladies
Lady Windermere's Fan
Life is a Dream
London Assurance
The Lower Depths
The Lucky Chance
Lulu
Lysistrata
The Malcontent
The Man of Mode
The Marriage of Figaro
Mary Stuart
The Master Builder
Medea
The Misanthrope
The Miser
Miss Julie
A Month in the Country
Oedipus
The Oresteia
Peer Gynt
Phedra
The Playboy of the Western World
The Recruiting Officer
The Revenger's Tragedy

The Rivals
The Roaring Girl
La Ronde
Rosmersholm
The Rover
Scapino
The School for Scandal
The Seagull
The Servant of Two Masters
She Stoops to Conquer
The Shoemakers' Holiday
Six Characters in Search of an Author
The Spanish Tragedy
Spring Awakening
Summerfolk
Tartuffe
Three Sisters
'Tis Pity She's a Whore
Too Clever by Half
Ubu
Uncle Vanya
Volpone
The Way of the World
The White Devil
The Wild Duck
A Woman of No Importance
Women Beware Women
Women of Troy
Woyzeck
Yerma

The publishers welcome suggestions for further titles

DRAMA CLASSICS

SIX CHARACTERS IN SEARCH OF AN AUTHOR

by
Luigi Pirandello

translated and introduced by
Stephen Mulrine

NICK HERN BOOKS
London
www.nickhernbooks.co.uk

A Drama Classic

Six Characters in Search of an Author first published in Great Britain
in this translation as a paperback original in 2003
by Nick Hern Books Limited, 14 Larden Road, London W3 7ST

Reprinted 2005, 2008, 2009

Typeset by Country Setting, Kingsdown, Kent CT14 8ES
Printed by CPI Bookmarque, Croydon

A CIP catalogue record for this book is available from
the British Library

ISBN 978 1 85459 089 3

Introduction

Luigi Pirandello (1867-1936)

Pirandello was born on 28 June 1867 in Sicily, near the
coastal town of Girgenti (Agrigento) in a farmhouse known
locally by the dialect word for 'chaos', an irony which the
playwright himself, now regarded as the pioneer dramatist of
modern man's existential dilemma, did not fail to remark.
Sicily at the time of Pirandello's birth was in the process of
coming to terms with the cataclysmic events of Italy's
transformation from a number of independent states into
one entity, and indeed Pirandello's father and uncles had
been staunch supporters of Garibaldi, the great Italian
patriot and freedom fighter, a few years earlier. The heady
optimism of the Risorgimento (the movement committed to
the 'resurrection' of Italy) quickly faded, however, as the gulf
between the thriving industrialised north of the country, and
the impoverished south widened. Sicily in particular suffered
badly from neglect and corruption.

Sicily in Pirandello's day was decidedly backward, its society
almost feudal in character, one in which the most severe
codes of public behaviour and outward respectability
contrasted sharply with the primitive and often brutal reality
of daily life. Extreme poverty co-existed with very substantial
wealth, and the young Pirandello, whose father owned a
prosperous sulphur mine, was sufficiently sensitive to be
embarrassed by his own privileged position. The contrasting
sights and sounds of his native Sicily had a profound impact

on both him, and his later work, which constantly explores
the gap between appearance and reality. The lane behind
his family home, for example, was a favourite venue for
duelling, a practice his own father engaged in more than
once, and the corpses of those killed in defence of 'honour'
were a familiar sight. On one occasion, a horrified
Pirandello also observed a couple making love alongside a
corpse in the local mortuary. While the Sicily of his early
years may have been a cultural backwater, there is little
doubt that such experiences were formative.

In 1886, after a brief spell in the family sulphur business,
Pirandello entered the University of Palermo to study law and
philosophy and, the following year, went on to continue his
education first in Rome, then the University of Bonn, where
he was awarded a doctorate in 1891, for a thesis on the
development of his local Girgenti dialect, proof of the importance to Pirandello of his Sicilian roots. On his return to
Rome in 1893, Pirandello soon became embroiled in the
literary debates of the day, aligning himself with the *Verismo*
writers, led by Luigi Capuana, dedicated to an austere
naturalism, as opposed to the more rhetorical and symbolic
writings of Gabriele D'Annunzio and his followers. Pirandello's
earliest published work had been a collection of poems, but
he now turned to prose, and his first novel, *L'Esclusa* (The
Outcast, 1893), was followed by a further six, over his long
career, including the acknowledged masterpiece *Il fu Mattia
Pascal* (The Late Mattia Pascal, 1904), in addition to hundreds
of short stories, essays and reviews, and some forty-odd plays
– many of them adapted from his own prose works.

In 1894, Pirandello entered into a typically Sicilian arranged
marriage with the daughter of his father's business partner,

Antonietta Portulano, a young woman of limited education, whom he scarcely knew. Over the next few years, the couple had three children, but in 1904 the collapse of the family sulphur-mining business, owing to a disastrous flood, caused Antonietta to have a nervous breakdown, from which she never fully recovered. Pirandello had already taken a lecturing post at a women's teaching college in Rome, but now found himself forced to write for a living as well. Among his non-fiction works of this period was an important essay on humour, *L'Umorismo* (1908), setting out the playwright's belief that life is in constant flux, and every attempt to control it, the manifold illusions and 'masks' we adopt to deny that harsh reality, are ultimately futile. Pirandello's concept of humour, in which tragic and comic co-exist as points of view, arises from that paradox, and forms the aesthetic basis of all his mature work.

As if to prove his own thesis, while the publication of *Il fu Mattia Pascal* in 1904 had brought him international fame, his private life became a long drawn-out nightmare, as Antonietta's mental state deteriorated. Pirandello's teaching duties at the Istituto Superiore di Magisterio, where he was appointed Professor of Italian Language in 1908, were a particular source of friction, with Antonietta ceaselessly accusing him of having affairs with his female students. At her lowest ebb, she even accused him of incest with their daughter Lietta, whom she also suspected of trying to poison her. The unhappy Lietta was driven to attempt suicide in 1918, and the following year, with the agreement of their three children, Pirandello had Antonietta committed to a mental institution, where she remained until her death in 1959.

By 1916, Pirandello was already in late middle age, with a solid body of mainly prose works behind him, highly regarded both at home and abroad. He had tried his hand at drama, in his younger days, with only limited success, but his career as a dramatist was effectively launched in that year with the premières in Rome of two Sicilian dialect plays, *Pensaci, Giacomino!* (Think It Over, Giacomino!), and *Liolà*. Two more plays appeared in 1917, *Così è (se vi pare)* (Right You Are, If You Think So), and *Il piacere dell'onestà* (The Pleasure of Honesty). In 1918, Pirandello published a substantial collection of plays, titled *Maschere nude* (Naked Masks), and over the next decade devoted himself almost full-time to the theatre, with some forty-odd plays eventually to his credit, including the acknowledged masterpieces *Sei personaggi in cerca d'autore* (Six Characters in Search of an Author, 1921), and *Enrico IV* (Henry IV, 1922).

By 1922, Pirandello was earning enough from royalties to resign his professorship at the Istituto, and in September 1924, along with a group of fellow-enthusiasts, known as 'The Eleven', he took the first step towards creating a permanent repertory theatre in Italy, modelled on companies established elsewhere in Europe. The Teatro d'Arte, with Pirandello as artistic director, and the talented Marta Abba as leading lady, was initially based in Rome, and funded by a government grant, with Mussolini's approval. Pirandello in fact joined Mussolini's Fascist Party in 1924, and made little secret of his admiration for Italy's 'strong man', although it has been argued that he was motivated less by political conviction, than by practical necessity. The issue is a complex one, and while Pirandello at one point even distributed propaganda justifying Italy's invasion of

Abyssinia, to theatre audiences in New York, it is also known that his relationship with the Fascist regime steadily worsened, as its repressive character became clear.

Despite Mussolini's support, Pirandello's dream of an Italian national theatre was never realised, and the Teatro d'Arte ran into financial difficulties, though it had achieved worldwide fame, during its brief life (1925-28), through a series of highly acclaimed tours to the major European cities, and South America. After the failure of the Teatro d'Arte, Pirandello went into voluntary exile first in Berlin, where he lived for a time with Marta Abba, and later in Paris. He continued to write, and in 1929 he was elected to the newly created Accademia d'Italia. International honours included the Nobel Prize for Literature in 1934, though it is alleged that Mussolini, who had expected to win the Peace Prize for his attempts to bring Germany back into the European system of alliances, was not impressed. The truth of the matter is that while Mussolini clearly recognised the propaganda value of Pirandello's support, his independent views made him an embarrassment to the regime, and the playwright's last years were spent in increasing isolation.

Pirandello died of pneumonia in Rome on 10 December 1936, leaving precise instructions for the disposal of his mortal remains – no state funeral, just a simple cremation, and the return of his ashes to his Sicilian birthplace, which was eventually achieved in 1961. For the playwright who so compellingly dramatised the existential plight of modern man, painfully bereft of all the old certainties, not least identity, the *Contrada Caos* (literally 'District of Chaos'), is a fitting resting-place.

Six Characters in Search of an Author:
What Happens in the Play

As the audience enter the auditorium, they are confronted
by a darkened, almost bare stage. The curtains are open,
there is no scenery, apart from a piano, and a few chairs
and tables, and the general impression is of a theatre during
the 'dead' hours of daylight, into which the audience have
somehow ventured by mistake. When the house lights go
down, the Technician enters and begins hammering nails
into a plank of wood. The noise disturbs the Stage Manager,
who emerges from backstage to remonstrate with the
Technician, and several actors and actresses drift into the
theatre for a rehearsal of the play they are scheduled to
perform that evening – Pirandello's *Rules of the Game*. The
Actors pass the time in casual conversation until the
Director arrives, followed soon after by the Leading Lady,
late as usual.

The rehearsal eventually gets under way, with the Prompter
reading the directions aloud, and a debate immediately
ensues between the Director and the Leading Man on the
interpretation of Pirandello's text, which neither appears to
have much faith in. The rehearsal is then suddenly
interrupted by the entrance, through the auditorium, of six
strange individuals, a family of sorts, consisting of Father,
Mother, Son, Stepdaughter, and two small children. They
are in possession of a compelling story, they say, and are
seeking an author to represent it. The Director at first
dismisses them as lunatics, but the Father's subtle reasoning,
and the Stepdaughter's more overtly seductive appeal
gradually win the company round, and they agree to give
the intruders a hearing.

The six Characters, it is revealed, are the creation of an author who originally brought them to life, but chose not to develop them any further, so that they remain in a kind of creative limbo, desperate to attain the immortality of a truly finished work of art. Their story, as it emerges piecemeal from the sometimes contradictory accounts of the Father, Mother and Stepdaughter, is an intriguing one. In the pursuit of 'sound moral health', as he claims, the Father married a simple peasant woman, with whom he found it impossible to communicate, and when she gave birth to a son, he had the latter sent away to be brought up in the country. Later, when he realised how much better suited his wife was to his gentle and kindhearted secretary, he persuaded the couple to go away together and begin a new life in another part of town. He continues to observe them over the years, however, and when the lovers start their own family, he takes a keen interest in his Stepdaughter, waiting outside the school gate each day to see her emerge.

After he approaches her one day with a gift, the family become alarmed and move away out of his reach, so that the Father loses all contact with them. Some years later, the secretary dies, and the Mother, now with three children to support, is driven by extreme poverty to move back into town, where she finds work as a seamstress with a certain Madame Pace, whose fashionable dress shop is in fact a brothel. Unbeknown to the Mother, in order to ensure the family's survival, the Stepdaughter, now a young woman, is forced to entertain Madame Pace's male clients in the shop's infamous back room. As luck would have it, the Father is one of those clients, and the key event in the Characters' tragic history is the encounter between him and the

Stepdaughter, when his attempt to purchase her sexual services is interrupted in the nick of time by the horrified Mother. The Stepdaughter now has a hold over the Father, and uses her power to get the family into his house, where she virtually assumes control, much to the disgust of the first-born Son, who regards himself as the only legitimate heir, and the other children as bastards. This is the defining moment in the Characters' existence, and Pirandello's directions make that clear, recommending the use of masks to fix their expressions forever – the guilt-ridden Father, the vengeful Stepdaughter, the anguished Mother, and the resentful Son. The two younger children, who never speak, and whose fate will be revealed only later, seem permanently horrified by all that they have witnessed.

As their story unfolds, the Director is sufficiently intrigued to abandon the scheduled rehearsal, and agree to grant the Characters' earnest wish for completion, by transcribing their experience as they re-live it on stage for the company, to create the work of art which they believe is their destiny. The Director and the Characters accordingly go backstage to draft a scenario, while the Actors, equally intrigued, if a little sceptical, enjoy a short break.

When the action resumes, the Director orders a rough approximation of Madame Pace's back room to be set up on stage, and casts the play, assigning the key roles of Father and Stepdaughter to the Leading Man and Leading Lady. The Prompter gets ready to write out a working script in shorthand, as the Father and Stepdaughter re-enact their encounter for the Actors' benefit. The plan immediately runs into difficulties, however, as the Characters object to the way they are to be represented, and a furious argument ensues, which calls into question the very nature of the theatrical illusion. Almost out of patience, the Director is finally about to start the rehearsal, when he realises that he has made no provision for Madame Pace. The Father then mysteriously asks the Actresses to hang up their hats and coats, in order to create a working environment, as it were, for the dressmaker, and a comically grotesque caricature of Madame Pace suddenly appears out of nowhere, to the astonishment of the Director and Actors.

The re-enactment at last gets under way, with a whispered conversation between Madame Pace and the Stepdaughter, which prompts another heated debate about theatrical conventions, whereby even whispers must be audible, and the Father prepares to make his entrance. The Mother, silently observing up to this point, can endure it no longer, and attacks Madame Pace, who is forced to leave the stage. The Father and Stepdaughter then begin to re-enact their encounter, with the Prompter rapidly transcribing their dialogue, and after a few moments, the Director instructs the Leading Lady and Leading Man to replay the scene they have just witnessed, suitably modified for the stage. When the Actors do so, drawing on the stereotypes of their art, the result strikes the Stepdaughter as so false that she bursts out laughing. The Father also objects to being misrepresented, and the rehearsal dissolves into a furious row, as the theatre professionals stand on their dignity. As far as the Stepdaughter is concerned, however, the last straw is the Director's insistence that the true nature of the encounter, in the course of which she was persuaded to undress for the Father's benefit, cannot be presented to a theatre audience. Like the eternally guilt-ridden Father, the

Stepdaughter is fixed for all time in an implacable desire for vengeance, and she is not convinced by the Director's plea for ensemble balance. She is determined to relive the moment as it actually happened, culminating in the Mother's shriek of horror, when she broke in on the pair. And at the end of the Stepdaughter's narration, when the anguished Mother does so, the Director's excited declaration that this will be the curtain line of the first act, is misinterpreted by a stagehand as a call to lower the curtain, bringing the rehearsal to a premature conclusion.

When the curtain is raised after the interval, the stage is set for the climactic scene of the Characters' play, with an ornamental garden pond. The Stepdaughter questions the accuracy of the setting, pointing out that some of the crucial events took place inside the house, but the Director defends his right to make changes, for practical reasons, in order to maintain the theatrical illusion. This prompts a philosophical debate between the Father and the Director, on the very nature of reality, in the course of which the Father argues that the Characters are in fact more real than the Director himself, since human life is in constant flux, ever-changing, whereas fictional characters are permanent and immutable. The Father goes on to discuss the creative process, claiming that once brought to life, characters are independent of their author, and describes the futile efforts he and the other Characters, especially the Stepdaughter, made to persuade their creator to realise them in a finished work of art.

The Director eventually overcomes the Stepdaughter's objections to the setting, and a compromise is agreed, whereby the Little Girl is to be shown happily playing in the garden, while her brother, the silent and brooding Young

Boy, will be concealed behind some shrubbery. To that end, the Director orders two small cypress trees to be lowered from the flies, along with a sky-cloth. Moonlight effects are added for atmosphere, and the stage is ready for action. Before the family's tragedy can be concluded, however, the Son must re-enact his scene with the Mother, and this he resolutely refuses to do, claiming that he is not involved in the drama, although the Stepdaughter insists that it was his rejection of the Mother, and the latter's obsessive need to justify her 'abandoning' him, her first-born, all those years ago, which brought about the tragedy. The Son even tries to leave the stage, but some mysterious force restrains him, and he ends up wrestling with the Father, who is determined to make him hear the distraught Mother's plea for forgiveness. Before that can happen, however, the Stepdaughter organises the various elements of the forthcoming tragedy – the Little Girl playing innocently beside the pond, the strange, psychologically-damaged Young Boy, with a loaded revolver in his pocket . . .

The Son is eventually forced to re-enact the harrowing scene in the garden, during which the Little Girl is accidentally drowned in the pond, while her brother looks on from his hiding-place behind the cypresses, motionless and seemingly dumbstruck with horror. As this scene is being played out on stage, a shot rings out; the Young Boy has committed suicide, and the Characters and Actors rush to investigate. The Young Boy's body is carried off-stage, but when the Actors return, no-one can be certain whether the suicide is real or pretended, and the rehearsal ends in confusion, with the Director complaining bitterly about the time he has wasted. When he calls for the lights to be switched off, however, the backcloth is suddenly illuminated with an eerie greenish light, and the silhouettes of the Characters, with the Little Girl and Young Boy significantly absent, are projected upon it. The Father, Mother, and Son then appear from behind the backcloth and stand motionless in centre stage, as if in a trance. Lastly, the Stepdaughter emerges, bursts into raucous laughter, and rushes out through the auditorium, laughing still.

Pirandello and the Theatre

Italian theatre companies in the late-nineteenth century were for the most part made up of actors who had been engaged to play specific role types, from one play to the next, and generally also itinerant. Prior to the unification of Italy, only a very few companies – those enjoying royal patronage, and a monopoly in their own cities, Milan and Naples, for example – had a settled base, to allow adequate rehearsal time. After 1860, while the changed political circumstances levelled the playing-field, so to speak, the financial pressures on companies entirely self-financed meant that success was often dependent on the drawing power at the box office of the leading actor, the *capocomico,* who was also responsible for the general management of the company. Apart from dis-couraging innovation, such a system was clearly open to abuse, and plays were not uncommonly distorted, with supporting roles reduced to a bare minimum in order to showcase the leading actor's talents. The great Eleanora Duse, for example, is said to have remained silent on stage for minutes at a time, to impose her presence on the audience.

Italy furthermore had produced no major playwrights since Goldoni, in the mid-eighteenth century; the standard repertoire was dominated by bourgeois melodrama and farce. A strand of socially-concerned plays, inspired by *Verismo* writers such as Giovanni Verga, won Pirandello's support initially, as an alternative to the grandiose neo-romantic theatre of Gabriele D'Annunzio, but the most productive influence on his own dramatic writing was the *teatro del grottesco*, as represented by Rosso di San Secondo and Luigi Chiarelli, whose work, like Pirandello's, explores the gap between appearance and reality, and the potentially tragicomic nature of all human transactions.

Pirandello was, however, also interested in dialect theatre, and his first successful venture into drama, following the disappointments of his youth, came about almost by chance, when his fellow Sicilian, the playwright and producer Nino Martoglio, staged two of his one-act plays, *La Morsa* (The Vice), and *Lumie di Sicilia* (Sicilian Limes), in Rome, in December 1910. Through Martoglio, Pirandello also met the impresario Angelo Musco, for whom he wrote several more Sicilian plays – *Pensaci, Giacomino!* (Think It Over, Giacomino!), *Il berretto a sonagli* (Cap and Bells), *Liolà*, and *La giara* (The Jar) – all successfully premièred in Rome, over the period 1916-17. These were swiftly followed by *Così è (se vi pare)* (Right You Are, If You Think So), *Il piacere dell'onestà* (The Pleasure of Honesty), and *Il giuoco delle parti* (The Rules of the Game), adapted, like many of Pirandello's plays, from earlier prose works, and demonstrating not only his growing confidence in the medium, but also a marked shift away from realism, to more searching philosophical concerns.

By 1921, plays by Pirandello were being performed all over Italy, but the première, in May of that year at the Teatro Valle, of *Sei personaggi in cerca d'autore* (Six Characters in Search of an Author), infuriated the Roman audience to such an extent that it was almost booed off the stage, with cries of *'Manicomio!'* ('Madhouse!'), and Pirandello barely escaped the theatre without injury. A few months later, after the play had been published, it was staged again at the Teatro Manzoni in Milan, before a well-prepared audience, and given a triumphant reception. *Six Characters in Search of an Author* went on to repeat its success in every major city in Europe, and by 1925 it had been translated into some twenty-five languages. Despite its initial failure in Rome, Pirandello had sufficient confidence in the play to begin work almost immediately on *Enrico IV* (Henry IV), and in 1923 his international fame was confirmed with a 'Pirandello season' at the Fulton Theater in New York, and significant productions of *Six Characters in Search of an Author* in Paris, by Georges Pitoëff, and in Berlin, by Max Reinhardt.

In 1924, Pirandello's lately re-awakened enthusiasm for the theatre bore fruit in the founding of the Teatro d'Arte, based in Rome, at the Teatro Odescalchi, and supported by Mussolini initially to the tune of some 500,000 lire. The renovation of the theatre alone, however, cost almost half that, and its limited capacity, a mere 300, meant that the company was forced to tour for much of its existence, albeit to worldwide acclaim. Pirandello's plans for the new venture, modelled on art theatres such as that of Stanislavsky in Moscow, laid heavy emphasis on lengthy rehearsal times, detailed analysis of text, and innovative scenic design. Mainstream Italian theatre was still in thrall to the star-system, at the expense of the ensemble, and the punishing tour schedule companies had to endure meant that actors had little or no time to learn their lines. As a consequence, the prompter spoke all the dialogue aloud, even during performance, frequently drowning out the actors! This Pirandello was determined to change, and to a great extent he succeeded. Certainly, alternatives to the outmoded actor-manager system existed, not least in the radical theatre of Marinetti and the Futurists. Their confrontational style and cavalier attitude to text, however, were at odds with Pirandello's vision, and it is his more cerebral challenge to the theatrical illusion which has proved its staying power.

Pirandello went on to interrogate the theatre in two more plays, *Ciascuno a suo modo* (Each in His Own Way, 1924), and *Questa sera si recita a soggetto* (Tonight We Improvise, 1930), closely linked to *Six Characters in Search of an Author* both structurally, in that each revolves around the creation of a play within the play, counterpointing dramatic action with analysis and commentary; and thematically, as Pirandello obsessively explores the concepts of identity and personality, multiple viewpoints, and the relativity of truth.

Pirandello was not without his critics in Italy, and the term *pirandellismo,* applied pejoratively, carried overtones of wilful obscurity, a perverse delight in baffling audiences with theoretical challenges to their objective reality. Indeed, Pirandello makes the Director in *Six Characters in Search of an Author* express that widely held opinion, while bewailing the lack of 'a decent French play', as the company begin rehearsing *The Rules of the Game*. In his own voice, however, Pirandello maintained that intellectual debate could be infused with genuine passion on stage, and his best work assuredly proves the point.

Pirandello's status in Italy was much enhanced by international success, and although the playwright's relationship with his Italian critics was always a sensitive one, in part owing to political circumstances, he could reflect with some justice on his achievement in helping to change the direction of theatre both at home and abroad. Mussolini's invitation to Pirandello in 1926, to submit plans for the national theatre he had so long envisaged, may have come to nothing, but, in the longer term, Pirandello was instrumental in modernising Italian theatre, taking it beyond the limitations of *Verismo* realism on the one hand, and the aestheticism of D'Annunzio on the other.

Without a doubt, his contribution to European theatre in general has been even greater. Concepts hitherto chiefly of interest to philosophers, such as the impossibility of communication, and the meaninglessness of existence, which we disguise from ourselves by adopting a variety of masks or temporary identities, are brought vividly to life, like his own Six Characters, in his prose fiction and drama. That ironic self-consciousness, which is so deeply ingrained in modern literature, is present in Pirandello's work almost from the outset, and the manner in which he exaggerates the stereotypes of domestic drama, and burdens them with self-awareness, played an important part in attuning audiences to the later Absurdist and Existentialist drama, of such writers as Anouilh, Sartre, Beckett, Ionesco, Genet, Albee and Pinter.

Pirandello's Nobel Prize citation of 1934 made specific reference to the way in which he had brilliantly 'renewed the stage', but his popularity by then was already waning, and his last years were somewhat embittered by neglect. His later plays, many of them premièred by his former leading lady Marta Abba, who founded her own company, are generally acknowledged inferior to his mid-period work. In the 1950s, however, a new international audience discovered him as a precursor to the Absurdists, and plays such as *The Rules of the Game*, *Six Characters in Search of an Author*, and *Henry IV* were frequently revived. Out of Pirandello's vast dramatic canon, these latter are still the most often performed, though the emphasis has arguably shifted away from their philosophical content, to the insights they offer on the role of the artist, and the nature of the creative process. Finally, Pirandello's biographer, Gaspare Giudice, sums up the playwright's achievement in the words of T S Eliot, writing in 1952: 'Pirandello is a dramatist to whom all dramatists of my own and future generations will owe a debt of gratitude. He has taught us something about our own problems and has pointed to the direction in which we can seek a solution to them'.

Six Characters in Search of an Author: **Themes**

Pirandello's *Six Characters in Search of an Author* is a main source of the complex of ideas, one might almost say obsessions, which run through his work, and which were summed up by his contemporaries in the term *pirandellismo*. Reduced to essentials, truth is relative, never more than a point of view, and any attempt at mutual understanding is doomed to failure, founded as it is on language, notoriously open to subjective interpretation. Identity and personality are likewise illusions, and are merely the sum total of the various masks we adopt as the occasion demands, in a vain effort to arrest the constant, chaotic movement of life, and to impose some sort of meaningful order upon it. In the world of the play, that order is the permanence of art, which alone can guarantee immortality, and the Father is Pirandello's chief spokesman in this aesthetic debate, even as he is forced to relive his suffering – eternal guilt for his shameful actions, culminating in sexual advances made to his Stepdaughter – which fixes his identity for all time, as a work of art.

Pirandello's play is didactic, in a very real sense, and perhaps the clearest demonstration of this is the Father's challenge to the Director's own reality, on the grounds that it is subject to change, over time, unlike that of a created character. The logic of the Father's argument is flawless, but its delivery is also convincingly dramatic, a typical example of Pirandello's manner – logic infused with passion. Similarly, the tragic history of the Six Characters, recounted in detail, may indeed be 'narrative', and unsuited to performance, but the fact that it is open to divergent interpretations by the chief protagonists makes it a battleground – a dramatic focus for Pirandello's belief in the relativity of truth.

Viewed from another angle, *Six Characters in Search of an Author* is a sustained examination of the creative process itself, and when the Father and Stepdaughter describe their own genesis, they echo the words of Pirandello's preface to the 1925 revised edition of the play, in which he writes of the Characters appearing to him as in a dream, and insistently clamouring to be given artistic form. Pirandello also makes it clear, however, that he has no interest in 'history' for its own sake, and could find no philosophical meaning in the Characters' story, to justify its further development – in effect adopting the stance he assigns to their author in the play, who abandoned them to their unresolved fate.

While the outward design of *Six Characters in Search of an Author* is to create a play before the audience's very eyes, that process at a deeper level is demonstrated in the Characters themselves, and their realisation, ranging from the three-dimensional complexity of the Father, tragically aware of every last nuance of his situation, to the near-catatonic children, whose Mother's simple grief is scarcely more eloquent. Between these extremes, the Stepdaughter pursues her own vengeful agenda, mostly at the expense of the Father's credibility, but she lacks his superior self-awareness – something which the taciturn Son later exhibits in refusing to take part in the play, on the grounds that he is incomplete, as their original author evidently understood. Madame Pace, on the other hand, is complete to the point of caricature, and although she is introduced as an example of artistic creation in the making, it may be that Pirandello is here satirising the tradition of actor-driven theatre, typified by the *commedia dell'arte*, as distinct from that based on the primacy of the author's text.

Much of the comedy in *Six Characters in Search of an Author* derives from Pirandello's critique of Italian theatre as he found it. The playwright's voice is clearly audible in the argument over the chef's hat, during the rehearsal of *The Rules of the Game*, and again in the quibbles occasioned by the Actors' misreading of the script for the scene in Madame Pace's boutique. Pirandello was a stickler for accuracy, and in a theatre where the prompter routinely read the dialogue aloud, actors often neglected to learn their lines – a practice he himself did much to change.

The acting company, whose domain the Characters invade, are likewise typical of the old-fashioned Italian theatre of the day, with their rigid hierarchy of Leading Man and Lady, Juvenile Lead and Ingénue, and a preferred repertoire of imported French warhorses, instead of the 'avant-garde' Pirandello work they are rehearsing. In fact, the Characters' family melodrama is just the kind of fare they, and by implication their audiences, appreciate, and the Actors instinctively fall back on stereotyped patterns. Thus, the Leading Man knows precisely how an aged roué should address his intended victim; he could play the part blindfold, and that is why the Stepdaughter, and beyond her Pirandello, of course, find his performance so comically artificial. On a more serious note, the Stepdaughter has every right to complain at the self-censorship proposed by the Director over her undressing on stage, which will sentimentalise the entire event.

The Characters' other objections to the manner in which their story is to be represented are perhaps less well founded, and betray a lack of understanding of theatre, and its climate of illusion and necessary compromise. The live actor can never be an accurate copy of the original; the setting, at least before the introduction of the webcam and 'reality' TV, can only be a crude approximation; the sequence of events must be telescoped. Pirandello was openly critical of drama, often contrasting it with the novel, and the latter's superior capacity for nuance. However, a working life encompassing over forty plays rather gives the lie to his professed distaste for theatre, and his prose fiction is rich in dramatic dialogue.

The fact is, the Characters' play-within-a-play never gets off the ground – their fate remains unresolved, their story mere background narrative to two very brief, albeit powerful scenes, constantly interrupted by arguments about interpretation and *mise-en-scène*. Indeed, one might say that the Characters' story is even more confused by the attempt to stage it, since the failure of the Young Boy and Little Girl to appear in the closing tableau leaves the audience wondering if the children aren't perhaps dead after all – shot and drowned 'for real'. But of course how could that happen on the stage, with its fake cypress trees and artificial moonlight? And where does the Stepdaughter actually go, when she runs out through the auditorium into the streets?

Six Characters in Search of an Author has a chaotic, improvised feel throughout, and from the moment the stage carpenter is interrupted at his work, nothing appears to go to plan. The very act divisions come about as a consequence of whim or accident, while the movement of the performers, on and off the stage, through the auditorium, is bewilderingly unpredictable, and must have seemed even more so, played at the high speed which Pirandello himself favoured. In truth, though, while the Characters' embryonic play remains formless, *Six Characters in Search of an Author* is a masterly construction, conforming to a traditional exposition-complication-resolution pattern, with the conflict between the Characters and Actors the true drama, rather than anything else. Its sheer complexity of content, however, ranging from philosophical reasoning, to the most commonplace concrete detail, within a time frame in which past and present frequently overlap, tends to conceal Pirandello's disciplined artifice.

Six Characters in Search of an Author is an extremely clever piece of work, but it is also very powerful, with its intense psychological probing, and highly charged current of emotion. Biographical links to the author are not always reliable, but it is perhaps worth observing that the Father, who speaks for Pirandello in so many respects, admits to having married his 'Amalia' in search of 'sound moral health', and then to finding it impossible to communicate with her – an experience painfully similar to Pirandello's own, with the convent-educated Antonietta. And like the Son, cruelly removed from his mother to be reared by a peasant woman, Pirandello himself was sent away to a wet-nurse in early infancy, an event which appears to have left its mark on him. One might also recall that in one of the worst episodes of her mental illness, Antonietta accused Pirandello and her daughter Lietta of having committed incest – prompting the latter to a bungled suicide attempt – and it may be argued that the roots of the Father's shameful approach to the Stepdaughter run deep indeed.

Gaspare Giudice cites many passages of almost pure autobiography from Pirandello's fiction, but the connection between the playwright's life and that of the dysfunctional family in *Six Characters in Search of an Author* is one aspect of the creative process Pirandello chooses not to explore, perhaps with good reason. Like so much else in the piece, that remains mysterious, but it is surely a contributing factor to the power of Pirandello's brilliant play of ideas.

Six Characters in Search of Author in **Performance**

By the time of the disastrous Rome première of *Six Characters in Search of an Author*, Pirandello had already written some twenty plays, approximately half of his total dramatic output, and enjoyed a fair degree of success. One can perhaps appreciate the shock, therefore, experienced by the first-night audience at the Teatro Valle, entering the theatre to find a stage bare to the brick walls, and a carpenter setting to work, oblivious to their presence. According to the critic Adriano Tilgher, however, the audience reserved judgment until the third act, before launching a torrent of catcalling and jeering, and a few fights even broke out in the auditorium. Tilgher's favourable review of the play, published next day in *Il Tempo*, incidentally did Pirandello a great service, and the playwright's explanatory preface to the 1925 edition of *Six Characters in Search of an Author* owes much to the critic's perceptive analysis of Pirandello's work.

The play Tilgher saw in Rome, however, was rather less radical than the later version: there were no steps, for example, connecting the stage to the auditorium, and the Characters entered conventionally upstage, without masks, moreover. The third act also concluded with the Director simply dismissing his actors – no closing tableau of the Characters, no dramatic exit through the auditorium for the Stepdaughter.

Preceded by publication, *Six Characters in Search of an Author* fared much better in Milan later that year, but its international career began in London, on 27 February 1922, with a private production by the Stage Society at the Kingsway Theatre. A professional performance had already

been banned by the Lord Chamberlain, on the grounds of
obscenity, and it took all of George Bernard Shaw's
persuasive powers to get it staged at all, though it proved an
outstanding success, directed by Fyodor Komisarjevsky, and
enthusiastically reviewed in the London press.

The most important early productions of *Six Characters in
Search of an Author*, however, apart from the playwright's own,
were undertaken in Paris, by Georges Pitoëff, and in Berlin,
by Max Reinhardt. Of the two, the Pitoëff production,
premièred at the Théâtre des Champs-Elysées on 10 April
1923, was the more to Pirandello's liking, though Pitoëff
took a good many liberties with the play, for example
lowering the Characters onto the stage by means of a
scenery lift, bathed in green light, as if from some misty
realm of the imagination. Pirandello disliked the notion, but
Pitoëff was adamant, and the playwright eventually adopted
many of the director's other changes, particularly to the
ending of the play, though the Stepdaughter's exit, as
published in the revised version of 1925, which is the one
used for this translation, was Pirandello's own idea.

Pirandello was less impressed by Max Reinhardt's production, premièred at the Komödie Theater on 30 December
1924, and hugely successful, with a run of over 130
performances. Though he may have been influenced by its
dramatic lighting effects, Pirandello in general disagreed with
Reinhardt's interpretation, in which the Characters were on
stage in darkness from the start, before making their
entrance in bizarre costumes, on a treadmill device lit from
below. In the playwright's view, Reinhardt's Expressionist,
anti-realist treatment overplayed the Characters' non-human,
alien quality, and Pirandello's precise description of the

Characters in the 1925 text is to some extent a counter-measure to that approach, as indeed is their naturalistic entry through the auditorium, again Pirandello's own later modification, along with the steps leading up to the stage.

Pirandello's innovations, in addition to those he adopted from Pitoëff and Reinhardt, appeared in his Teatro d'Arte production of the play at the Odescalchi Theatre in Rome in the spring of 1925. This was performed in London, at the New Oxford Theatre, in June of that same year – in Italian, since the Lord Chamberlain had banned performances in English. Interestingly, the *Times* reviewer observed that it seemed more of a comedy than the Stage Society production a few years earlier. It was also noted that Pirandello's Actors appeared in everyday summer dress, whereas the Characters wore sombre, sculptural black for the most part – virtually the opposite of the Stage Society's version. The naturalistic performances of the Italians attracted much admiration, though a number of critics complained of the actors regularly being drowned out by the prompter – something Pirandello had yet to correct.

The Teatro d'Arte also toured the play to Berlin, where Pirandello's own production was compared rather unfavourably with that of Reinhardt the previous year, basically on the grounds that it lacked seriousness. Reinhardt had also emphasised the role of the Director, who played with his back to the audience throughout, which suggested that the Characters were a figment of his imagination.

Pirandello in the main tended to avoid spectacular effects, preferring to bring the play to life through the performers, whom he rehearsed in depth, applying both the Stanislavsky method of character analysis, and a freer, improvisatory technique adapted from the *commedia dell'arte*. Pirandello's company played at a fast pace and at great intensity, with the effect that their superficial naturalism was exaggerated almost to the point of parody.

The very nature of *Six Characters in Search of an Author* invites a wide variety of interpretations, and while Reinhardt's Director-centred approach remained influential in Germany, an important production in 1953, directed in Düsseldorf by Ulrich Erfurth, was much closer to Pirandello's own reading of the play, emphasising the essential humanity of Father and Stepdaughter, in contrast to the shallow 'professionals' charged with representing them.

Tyrone Guthrie's 1955 production at the New York Phoenix Theater, in addition to considerable rewriting, was also distinguished by some brilliant effects, including that of having Madame Pace disappear, like a pantomime demon, in a puff of smoke. Madame Pace also called for special treatment in a 1988 adaptation by Robert Brustein at the Joyce Theater, New York, where she was re-invented as a male Puerto Rican pimp!

Notable London productions include an earlier attempt by Tyrone Guthrie, at the Westminster Theatre in 1932, with Flora Robson as the Stepdaughter. Barbara Jefford played the same role in 1963, at the Mayfair Theatre, with Ralph Richardson as the Father, and many years later also played the Mother, with Ralph Fiennes as the Son, in Nicholas Wright's adaptation directed by Michael Rudman at the National Theatre in 1987. Among foreign companies presenting the play in London, since Pirandello's own production, the most notable are the Italian Compagnia dei Giovani in 1965, and Anatoly Vasiliev's Russian adaptation staged as part of the London International Festival of Theatre in 1989. Finally, an adaptation by David Harrower, titled *Six Characters Looking for an Author*, was well received at the Young Vic in 2001.

The question of adaptation is particularly fraught in the case of *Six Characters in Search of an Author*, and it has been said that much of the play's meaning is lost if it is now played as written, in a 1921 setting in which actresses turn up to rehearsals wearing hats, and doormen address directors as *'Commendatore'* – 'Your Honour'. At a deeper level, moreover, Madame Pace's little boutique-cum-brothel is no place for modern transactions of the sort envisaged by the Father, who would be more likely to use the services of a discreet hotel and an escort agency. Accordingly, that element of real world recognition, which was part of the shock experienced by Pirandello's first audiences, is impossible to replicate in a translation of the author's actual text.

Pirandello, who in practice fiercely resented any interference with the author's text, was nevertheless aware of the problem in theory, and perhaps the authoritative word on the subject should be his own, published in 1936 in an introductory essay to Silvio D'Amico's *Storia del teatro italiano*: 'Theatre is not archaeology. A reluctance to adapt old works in order to bring them up to date for a new production, betokens a lack of interest, and not commendable caution. Theatre needs to keep up with the times, and has constantly been revitalised by that process, in those periods when it was at its liveliest. The text will always remain intact for those who wish to read it at home, for their own enlightenment.

Those who wish to enjoy themselves will go to the theatre, where the text will be presented free of dead wood and outmoded expressions, and adapted to the tastes of the day'.

For Further Reading

Pirandello's complete works in Italian can be found in the six-volume edition by Mondadori, in the series *I Classici Contemporanei Italiani* (1956-60). The Italian text of *Six Characters in Search of an Author* is available, along with that of *Henry IV* and *The Jar*, in a collection edited for Manchester University Press (1974), by Felicity Firth, who also provides useful notes and an excellent introduction. Gaspare Giudice's standard biography of Pirandello, translated by Alastair Hamilton, published by Oxford University Press (1975), is immensely detailed and readable. Among critical writings, the volume *Pirandello* by Renate Matthaei in the World Dramatists series, published by Frederick Ungar, New York (1973), is well worth tracking down, as is *A Companion to Pirandello Studies*, edited by John Louis Di Gaetani, Greenwood Press, New York (1991), and *Understanding Luigi Pirandello*, by Fiora A. Bassanese, published by the University of South Carolina Press (1997). Pirandello's theatre practice is discussed at length in *Luigi Pirandello, Director*, by A. Richard Sogliuzzo, published by Scarecrow Press, Metuchen, New Jersey and London (1982), and also in the estimable *Luigi Pirandello in the Theatre: A Documentary Record*, edited by Susan Bassnett and Jennifer Lorch, Harwood Academic Publishers (1993). Finally, an impressively wide range of Pirandello themes is explored in *Luigi Pirandello: Contemporary Perspectives*, edited by Gian-Paolo Biasin and Manuela Gieri, and published by the University of Toronto Press (1999).

Pirandello: Key Dates

1867   28 June, Luigi Pirandello born at Il Caos, near Girgenti (Agrigento), Sicily.

1881   Family moves to Palermo. Pirandello attends high school, later university.

1887   Leaves Sicily to study at the University of Rome.

1889   Transfers to the University of Bonn, Germany.

1891   Awarded doctorate, for thesis on the Girgenti dialect.

1892-93 Teaches briefly at the University of Bonn, before moving to Rome.

1893   Publishes first novel, *L'esclusa* (The Outcast).

1893   Resident in Rome, meets Luigi Capuana, introduced to literary circles. Marries Antonietta Portulano, daughter of father's business partner. Publishes first collection of short stories.

1897   Takes up lecturing post at Istituto Superiore di Magisterio, women's teacher training college.

1903   Family sulphur-mining business destroyed by flooding. Antonietta has first nervous breakdown.

1904   Novel, *Il fu Mattia Pascal* (The Late Mattia Pascal) published.

1908   Novel, *I vecchi e i giovani* (The Old and the Young) published. Essay, *L'umorismo* (On Humour).

1910   Two Sicilian plays staged in Rome, *La morsa* (The Vice), and *Lumie di Sicilia* (Sicilian Limes).

1916   Premières in Rome of *Liolà*, and *Pensaci, Giacomino!* (Think It Over, Giacomino!).

1917   Premières in Rome of *Il berretto a sonagli* (Cap and Bells) and *La Giara* (The Jar); premières of *Così è (se vi pare)* (Right You Are (If You Think So) in Milan, and *Il piacere d'onestà* (The Pleasure of Honesty) in Turin.

1918   Première in Rome of *Il giuoco delle parti* (The Rules of the Game). Collection of plays, *Maschere nude* (Naked Masks) published.

1919   Wife Antonietta committed to sanatorium, where she died in 1959.

1921   10 May, première in Rome at Teatro Valle of *Sei personaggi in cerca d'autore* (Six Characters in Search of an Author).

1922   24 February, première in Milan of *Enrico IV* (Henry IV). *Vestire gli ignudi* (To Clothe the Naked) premièred in Rome. Resigns from teaching post at Istituto.

1922-37 Publication of *Novelle per anno* (Short Stories for a Year), in fifteen volumes.

1923   Paris première of *Six Characters in Search of an Author*, directed by Georges Pitoëff.

1924   Pirandello joins Fascist Party. Première in Milan of
        Ciascuno a suo modo (Each in His Own Way). Estab-
        lishes own theatre company, Teatro d' Arte, in Rome,
        with funding from Mussolini.

1925   Teatro d' Arte tours to England, France, Germany
        and the United States.

1926   Publishes last novel, *Uno, nessuno e centomila* (One,
        No-one and a Hundred Thousand). Mussolini
        invites Pirandello to submit plan for national
        theatre.

1927   Teatro d'Arte tours South America.

1928   Teatro d'Arte disbanded, through lack of financial
        support. Pirandello leaves Italy, resides in Berlin,
        then Paris, until 1933.

1929   Pirandello appointed to newly created Accademia
        d'Italia.

1930   Première in Königsberg of *Questa sera si recita a
        soggetto* (Tonight We Improvise).

1934   Première of opera, *La favola del figlio cambiato* (The
        Fable of the Changeling Son), in Braunschweig,
        Hitler in attendance. Pirandello receives Nobel
        Prize for Literature.

1936   Pirandello dies in Rome of pneumonia, 10
        December. Final play, *I giganti della montagna* (The
        Mountain Giants) unfinished, staged posthumously.

SIX CHARACTERS
IN SEARCH OF AN AUTHOR

Characters in the play about to be made

THE FATHER
THE MOTHER
THE STEPDAUGHTER
THE SON
THE YOUNG BOY (non-speaking)
THE LITTLE GIRL (non-speaking)
MADAME PACE (conjured up later in the play)

Actors in the company

THE DIRECTOR
THE LEADING LADY
THE LEADING MAN
THE SECOND ACTRESS
THE INGENUE
THE JUVENILE LEAD
OTHER ACTORS AND ACTRESSES
THE STAGE MANAGER
THE PROMPTER
THE PROPS MAN
THE TECHNICIAN
THE DIRECTOR'S SECRETARY
THE DOORMAN
STAGEHANDS, ETC.

The action takes place during the daytime, on the stage of a theatre. There are no act or scene divisions, but the performance is interrupted twice, on the first occasion without lowering the curtain, when the DIRECTOR *and the leading character, i.e. the* FATHER, *withdraw to rough out the scenario, and the* ACTORS *leave the stage; on the second occasion, when the* TECHNICIAN *lowers the curtain by mistake.*

The audience enters the theatre to find the curtain already raised, and the stage looking as it does during the day, with no wings or scenery, almost completely dark and empty, so that they have the impression of an impromptu performance from the outset.

Two small flights of steps, one at right, the other at left, serve to connect the stage with the auditorium. On the stage, the cover of the prompt-box has been removed, and stands to one side. Downstage at the other side, stand a small table and a chair with its back to the audience, for the DIRECTOR. *Two more tables, one larger, one smaller, and several chairs, are also downstage, ready for the rehearsal, if required. There are other chairs, scattered around left and right, for the* ACTORS. *Upstage to one side is a piano, partly hidden.*

When the house lights go down, the TECHNICIAN *enters from the upstage door in dark blue overalls with a tool-bag hung from his belt; from a corner upstage he gathers a few planks, takes them downstage, and kneels down to begin nailing them together. While the hammering is going on, the* STAGE MANAGER *rushes in, through the door leading to the dressing-rooms.*

STAGE MANAGER. Hey! What are you doing?

TECHNICIAN. What d'you think I'm doing? I'm knocking in nails.

STAGE MANAGER. At this time? (*Looks at his watch.*) It's half-past ten already. The director'll be here any minute for the rehearsal.

TECHNICIAN. Look, I've got to have time to do *my* work as well!

STAGE MANAGER. Well, you can have it, but not now.

TECHNICIAN. All right, when?

STAGE MANAGER. When we're finished rehearsing. Now come on, clear all this out of the way and let me set up the stage for Act Two of *Rules of the Game*.

The TECHNICIAN, *breathing heavily and muttering, picks up the planks and goes off. Meanwhile, the* ACTORS *of the company, male and female, begin to drift in through the stage door, in ones and twos, random-fashion – nine or ten, presumably as many as are required for the rehearsal of Pirandello's play* The Rules of the Game, *scheduled for that day. They enter, greet the* STAGE MANAGER, *and exchange pleasantries. Some make their way to the dressing-rooms; others, including the* PROMPTER, *who carries a rolled-up copy of the script under his arm, hang around the stage, waiting for the* DIRECTOR *to start the rehearsal. In the interim, sitting or standing in groups, they talk amongst themselves; one lights up a cigarette, one complains about his role in the play, another reads out some news item from a theatre journal. Ideally, the* ACTORS *and* ACTRESSES *will be wearing light-coloured, casual clothing, and this first improvised scene should have a lively, natural feel. At a certain point, one of the cast sits down at the piano and plays a dance-tune; some of the younger* ACTORS *and* ACTRESSES *begin dancing.*

STAGE MANAGER (*clapping his hands to call them to order*). Right, that's enough, everybody! The director's here.

The music and dancing suddenly stop. The ACTORS *turn to look out into the auditorium, as the* DIRECTOR *enters through the rear door. He walks down the central aisle with his hat firmly planted on his head, a cane under his arm, and a huge cigar in his mouth. As the cast greet him, he mounts the stage by one of the two little staircases; his* SECRETARY *hands him his mail: a few newspapers, and a bound script.*

DIRECTOR. No letters?

SECRETARY. No. That's all there is.

DIRECTOR (*handing him back the script*). Put it in my office.

He then looks around and turns to the STAGE MANAGER.

I can't see a thing here. Let's have some light, please.

STAGE MANAGER. Right.

He goes to give the order, and after a moment the stage right area, where the ACTORS *are standing, is illuminated with a bright white light. Meanwhile, the* PROMPTER *has taken up position in his box, switched on his lamp, and spread the script out in front of him.*

DIRECTOR (*clapping his hands*). Right, come on – let's make a start. (*To the* STAGE MANAGER.) Is anyone missing?

STAGE MANAGER. Our leading lady.

DIRECTOR. As usual! (*Looks at his watch.*) We're ten minutes late already. Make a note of that, if you will, please. She really must learn to be on time for rehearsals.

He has barely finished his reprimand when the LEADING LADY's *voice is heard at the rear of the auditorium.*

LEADING LADY. Oh, for heaven's sake! I'm here, I'm here!

She is dressed all in white, with an audacious hat on her head, and a little lap-dog under her arm. She rushes down the central aisle and hurriedly climbs on stage by one of the little staircases.

DIRECTOR. You've obviously made a vow to keep us waiting the whole day.

LEADING LADY. I'm sorry. I tried very hard to get here on time, but I just couldn't find a taxi! Anyway, I can see you haven't started yet, and I'm not on straight away.

She calls the STAGE MANAGER *by name, and hands him the little dog.*

Put him in my dressing-room for me, there's a dear.

DIRECTOR (*muttering*). And her lap-dog next! As if we haven't enough dogs already!

He claps his hands again and turns to the PROMPTER.

Right, then – *Rules of the Game,* Act Two. (*Sits in his armchair.*) Let's have your attention, everybody! Who's on stage?

The ACTORS *and* ACTRESSES *clear the front of the stage and sit to one side, except for the three who are to start the rehearsal, and the* LEADING LADY, *who ignores the* DIRECTOR's *request, and sits down in front at one of the little tables.*

DIRECTOR (*to the* LEADING LADY). So you *are* in this scene?

LEADING LADY. Who, me? No, sir.

DIRECTOR (*annoyed*). Then get off, for heaven's sake!

The LEADING LADY *stands up and walks over to sit with the other* ACTORS, *who have already moved to one side.*

DIRECTOR (*to the* PROMPTER). Right, let's get on with it.

PROMPTER (*reading from the script*). 'In the house of Leone Gala. An unusual room, serving as both dining-room and study . . . '

DIRECTOR (*turning to the* STAGE MANAGER). We'll use the red room set.

STAGE MANAGER (*making a note on a piece of paper*). The red. That's fine.

PROMPTER (*continuing to read from the script*). 'The table is laid, and there is a writing-desk with books and papers; bookcases and cabinets with expensive china and table-ware. An exit upstage to Leone's bedroom; an exit left to the kitchen; main exit at right . . . '

DIRECTOR (*standing up and pointing*). Now, pay attention, everybody: over there, the main exit – over here, the kitchen. (*Turning to the* ACTOR *who is to play the part of Socrates.*) You'll enter and exit from here. (*To the* STAGE MANAGER.) We'll have the inner door at the back, and put some curtains on it. (*Returns to his seat.*)

STAGE MANAGER (*making a note*). Right.

PROMPTER (*reading, as before*). 'Scene One – Leone Gala, Guido Venanzi, Filippo, known as Socrates . . . ' (*To the* DIRECTOR.) Do I have to read the actors' directions as well?

DIRECTOR. Yes, of course! I've told you a hundred times!

PROMPTER (*reading, as before*). 'When the curtain rises, Leone Gala, wearing a chef's hat and apron, is busy beating an egg in a bowl with a wooden spoon. Filippo, similarly dressed as a cook, is beating another egg. Guido Venanzi is sitting listening to them . . . '

LEADING MAN (*to the* DIRECTOR). Excuse me, but do I really have to wear a chef's hat?

DIRECTOR (*irked by the question*). I imagine so. I mean, it *is* in the script! (*Pointing to it.*)

LEADING MAN. Well, I'm sorry, but it's a bit silly.

DIRECTOR (*leaping up in a rage*). Silly? Silly? Well, what am I expected to do if we can't get hold of a decent French play, and we're reduced to putting on this Pirandello stuff – fine if you can understand him, but they're written that way deliberately so nobody likes them – neither actors, critics, or audiences!

The ACTORS *laugh. The* DIRECTOR *then gets up, goes over to the* LEADING MAN *and begins shouting.*

So, the chef's hat – yes! And beat those eggs! What, d'you think that's all you're doing – just beating a simple egg? Well, I've got news for you. Those egg-shells you're beating are supposed to be symbolic!

The ACTORS *start to laugh again, and make ironic comments to one another.*

Be quiet, there! And listen while I'm trying to explain. (*Turning again to the* LEADING MAN.) Now, sir – the egg-shell: it's meant to represent the outer form of reason, emptied of its content, which is blind instinct! You're reason, and your wife is instinct, you're involved in a game, playing a part you've been assigned, and you consciously become your own puppet. D'you understand?

LEADING MAN (*spreading his hands*). Frankly, no.

DIRECTOR (*returning to his place*). Neither do I. Anyway, let's crack on. You'll like how it turns out. (*Confidentially.*) By the way, I think you should face about three-quarters on, otherwise what with the obscure dialogue, and the fact the audience won't hear you, the whole thing'll die the death. (*Clapping his hands again.*) Right, everybody, let's do it!

PROMPTER. Excuse me, sir – is it all right if I get into my box? There's a bit of a draught here.

DIRECTOR. Yes, yes, of course. Do so.

Meanwhile, the DOORMAN, *in his gold-braided cap, has entered the auditorium and walked down the central aisle towards the stage, to inform the* DIRECTOR *of the arrival of the* SIX CHARACTERS, *who have followed him into the auditorium, and now stand a little way off, looking around them. They seem puzzled and disorientated.*

In staging this play, every effort should be made not to confuse these SIX CHARACTERS *with the* ACTORS. *The positioning of the two groups on the stage (indicated in the directions) will undoubtedly help, as will different-coloured lighting. However, the most apt and effective suggestion is the use of special masks for the* CHARACTERS: *masks made for the purpose, from material which will not go limp from perspiration, yet light enough for the actors to wear easily; they must also be cut and shaped in such a way as to leave the eyes, nose and mouth free. This will also bring* out the underlying meaning of the play. The CHARACTERS, in fact, should not appear as unreal beings, but rather as created reality, immutable constructs of the imagination, and therefore more real and substantial than the naturally changeable ACTORS. The masks will help to give the impression of figures created by art, each one fixed for all time in its fundamental emotion, i.e. for the FATHER, remorse; for the STEPDAUGHTER, revenge; for the SON, contempt; for the MOTHER, sorrow. Thus, her mask will have wax tears permanently attached under the dark hollows of her eyes and down her cheeks, like those to be seen on paintings and statues of the Mater Dolorosa in churches. Also her dress should be very plain, but of a special shape and material, with stiff folds and an almost sculptural appearance; in sum, the impression should be of something not to be found in any city store, or made up by any dressmaker.

The FATHER is about fifty, with reddish hair thinning at the temples, but not bald; a full moustache curls around his still youthful mouth, which frequently opens in a diffident and vacant smile. He is pale, especially noticeable on his ample forehead; his blue, oval-shaped eyes are bright and piercing; he wears light-coloured trousers and a dark jacket; his voice is sometimes caressing, at other times harsh and abrupt.

The MOTHER appears frightened, and crushed by an intolerable burden of shame and humiliation. She is dressed simply in widow's weeds, with a thick crêpe veil, and when she lifts her veil, we see an unlined, almost waxen face, her eyes constantly downcast.

The STEPDAUGHTER, eighteen years old, is arrogant to the point of insolence. She is very beautiful, also dressed in mourning, but conspicuously elegant. She is clearly contemptuous of the timid and pitifully confused demeanour of her brother, a scruffy-looking YOUNG BOY of fourteen, likewise dressed all in black; on the other hand, she exhibits warm affection for her sister, a LITTLE

GIRL *of about four, wearing a white dress with a black silk sash around the waist.*

The SON, *twenty-two years old, is tall, and somewhat rigid in his display of contempt for the* FATHER, *and sullen indifference towards the* MOTHER. *He wears a mauve-coloured overcoat, with a long green scarf round his neck.*

DOORMAN (*with his cap in his hand*). Excuse me, your honour.

DIRECTOR (*testily*). What is it now?

DOORMAN (*hesitantly*). Sir – there's some people here . . . they're asking to see you.

The DIRECTOR *and the* ACTORS *turn to look out into the auditorium, astonished.*

DIRECTOR (*enraged again*). Look, this is a rehearsal! You know perfectly well nobody's allowed in during rehearsals! (*Peering into the auditorium.*) Who are you people? What do you want?

The FATHER *advances as far as one of the staircases leading up to the stage, and the others follow him.*

FATHER. We're here in search of an author.

DIRECTOR (*startled and angry*). An author? What author?

FATHER. Any author, sir.

DIRECTOR. There's no author here – it's not a new play we're doing.

STEPDAUGHTER (*pleased and excited, rushing up the steps*). That's all the better – that's so much better, sir! We can be your new play!

AN ACTOR (*amid witty comments and laughter from the other* ACTORS). Just listen to that!

FATHER (*following the* STEPDAUGHTER *onto the stage*). Yes, but if there's no author . . . (*To the* DIRECTOR.) Unless you wouldn't mind . . .

The MOTHER, *holding the* LITTLE GIRL *by the hand, and the* YOUNG BOY *climb the first few steps and wait there. The* SON *remains below, sulking.*

DIRECTOR. Is this some sort of a joke?

FATHER. No, how can you say that, sir? On the contrary, we're bringing you a truly painful tragedy.

STEPDAUGHTER. We could even make your fortune for you!

DIRECTOR. Look, do me a favour and clear off. We don't have time to waste on lunatics.

FATHER (*offended, but pleasantly*). Oh, my dear sir, I'm sure you're well aware that life is full of endless absurdities, which may be quite blatant, but don't even have to seem plausible, for the very fact that they're true.

DIRECTOR. What the devil's he on about?

FATHER. What I'm saying, sir, is that it may actually be a form of madness to do the opposite, and strain to create plausible situations, to make them appear true. But allow me to observe, sir, that if this is madness, then it's nonetheless the entire *raison d'être* of your profession.

The ACTORS *react indignantly.*

DIRECTOR (*standing up and glaring at him*). I see. So you think our profession's full of lunatics, is that it?

FATHER. Well, if you try to make something seem true when it isn't . . . And not out of necessity either, sir – for fun . . . I mean, isn't it your job to give life on stage to imaginary characters?

DIRECTOR (*quickly, voicing the rising indignation of the* ACTORS). I'll have you know, my dear sir, that the actor's profession is a truly noble calling! Even if these new playwrights nowadays give us nothing but stupid comedies to act, playing puppets instead of human beings, then know this, sir – we can still boast of having given life to some immortal works – yes, on these very boards!

The ACTORS, *satisfied, show their approval by applauding the* DIRECTOR.

FATHER (*interrupting, and vehemently pressing home his point*). There, you see? That's excellent! To be alive – more alive than the kind of people who breathe and wear clothes! Not as real, perhaps, but more true. We're in complete agreement, don't you see?

The ACTORS *look at each other, astonished.*

DIRECTOR. Now, wait a minute – you actually said . . .

FATHER. No, I'm sorry, sir – I only said that because you were shouting about having no time to waste on lunatics. And I mean, nobody knows better than yourself how Nature uses the human imagination, to pursue her creative work to an even higher level.

DIRECTOR. Yes, all right, all right. But where does that get us?

FATHER. Nowhere, sir. It just shows that we can be born to life in so many ways, so many forms: as a tree or a stone, water or a butterfly . . . or a woman. And you can be born as a character too!

DIRECTOR (*with ironic feigned surprise*). So you, and all these other people, have been born as characters?

FATHER. Precisely, sir. And alive, as you can see.

The DIRECTOR *and* ACTORS *burst out laughing, as if at a joke. The* FATHER *is offended.*

I'm sorry you think that's funny, because we bear within us, I can only repeat, a truly painful tragedy, as you may perhaps be able to deduce from the presence of this lady dressed in black.

As he says this, he offers his hand to the MOTHER *and helps her up the last few steps; then, continuing to hold her hand, he conducts her with an air of tragic solemnity to the far side of the stage, which is suddenly illuminated by an eerie light. The* LITTLE GIRL *and the* YOUNG BOY *follow the* MOTHER; *next the* SON, *who stands to one side, upstage; the* STEPDAUGHTER *then follows, and moves apart to stand downstage, leaning against the proscenium arch. The* ACTORS, *initially astonished, then impressed by this development, break into applause, as if they had just witnessed a performance staged for their benefit.*

DIRECTOR (*initially bewildered, then indignant*). Good heavens! That's enough – be quiet! (*Turning to the* CHARACTERS.) And you people, clear off! Go away! (*To the* STAGE MANAGER.) For God's sake, get rid of them!

STAGE MANAGER (*comes forward, then stops, as if held back by some strange feeling of fear*). Go away! Please go away!

FATHER (*to the* DIRECTOR). No no, you see, we have
to . . .

DIRECTOR (*shouting*). Now look here – we've got work to do!

LEADING MAN. This isn't right – you can't mess us about
like this . . .

FATHER (*resolute, advancing*). Gentlemen, I really do wonder
at your incredulity! Maybe you're not used to seeing
characters spring to life up here, one after another –
characters created by an author? Or maybe it's because
we're not contained in a script? (*Indicates the prompt-box.*)

STEPDAUGHTER (*moves towards the* DIRECTOR, *smiling
seductively*). Believe me, sir, we truly are six of the most
fascinating characters. Even if we *have* lost our way.

FATHER (*brushing her aside*). Yes, lost our way, that's
absolutely right. (*To the* DIRECTOR, *quickly.*) In the sense
that the author who created us, gave us life, then either
didn't want to, or wasn't able to employ us in a work
of art. And that's criminal, sir, because if you're lucky
enough to be born alive as a character, well, you've
nothing to fear from death. You can't ever die. The man
will die, the author, the instrument of creation, yes, but
the creation itself never dies! And in order to live forever,
it needn't have any extraordinary gifts, or the ability to
work miracles. I mean, who was Sancho Panza? Who
was Don Quixote? They'll live forever, even so, because
their seeds, as it were, had the good fortune to fall on
fertile ground – an imagination that knew how to grow
and nourish them, and make them live for all eternity!

DIRECTOR. That's all very well, but what exactly do you
want here?

FATHER. We want to live, sir!

DIRECTOR (*ironically*). For all eternity?

FATHER. No, sir. Just for a moment – in you.

AN ACTOR. D'you hear that?

LEADING LADY. They want to live, in us!

JUVENILE LEAD (*indicating the* STEPDAUGHTER). That's fine by me, as long as I get her.

FATHER. Now look, look – the play's still got to be written. (*To the* DIRECTOR.) But if you and your actors are willing, we can sort out the plot between us right now!

DIRECTOR (*testily*). Sort what out? We don't go in for plots here. We put on serious plays and comedies.

FATHER. That's right! And that's precisely why we've come to you!

DIRECTOR. And where's the script?

FATHER. It's here, sir – in us. (*The* ACTORS *laugh.*) The play's in us, we're the play, and we're desperate to present it – it's as if there's a passion inside driving us on!

STEPDAUGHTER (*scornfully, adopting an exaggeratedly suggestive pose*). Oh, sir, if you only knew my passion! My passion . . . is for him!

She indicates the FATHER, *and makes as if to embrace him, then starts shrieking with laughter.*

FATHER (*in a fit of anger*). You keep out of this, d'you hear! And stop that laughing!

STEPDAUGHTER. Oh, really? Well, then, sirs – even

though I've been an orphan for a mere two months – let me show you how I can sing and dance!

With an air of malice, she begins singing 'Prends garde à Tchou-Tchin-Tchou' (English version 'Chu-Chin-Chow') by Dave Stamper, arranged as a foxtrot or slow one-step by Francis Salabert; she sings the first verse, accompanied with a few dance steps.

In a fairy book a Chinese crook
Has won such wondrous fame
That nowadays he appears in plays
And Chu-Chin-Chow's his name . . .

While she is singing and dancing, the ACTORS, *especially the young ones, appear strangely spellbound by her, and begin edging towards her, their arms outstretched as if to seize hold of her. She gives them the slip, and when the* ACTORS *burst into applause, and the* DIRECTOR *rebukes them, she remains aloof, deep in thought.*

ACTORS AND ACTRESSES (*laughing and applauding*). Bravo! Well done! Excellent!

DIRECTOR (*angrily*). Be quiet! What d'you think this is, a cabaret? (*Taking the* FATHER *to one side, anxiously.*) Look, what's the matter with her – is she mad?

FATHER. No, not mad. Worse!

STEPDAUGHTER (*rushing up to the* DIRECTOR). Worse? Worse? And the rest, sir! It's worse, all right. Just listen – please. Let's put this play on right away, and you'll see how at a certain point – when this little darling here . . .

She takes the hand of the LITTLE GIRL, *who is standing beside the* MOTHER, *and leads her up to the* DIRECTOR.

Look how pretty she is! (*Picks her up and kisses her.*) There, sweetheart!

Puts her back down, and continues, now deeply moved, almost against her will.

Anyway, when God suddenly decides to take this little darling away from this poor mother, and this idiot here . . .

Thrusts the YOUNG BOY *forward, grabbing him roughly by the sleeve.*

. . . does the stupidest thing, like the idiot he is . . .

Pushes him back towards the MOTHER.

You won't see me for dust! No, sir! I'm clearing off! Right out of it! I can hardly wait, I'm telling you. Because after that intimate little episode between me and him . . .

With a lewd wink in the direction of the FATHER.

. . . I can't stay here a minute longer with these people, watching this mother go through agonies on account of that queer fish over there –

Points at the SON.

Just look at him! Couldn't care less, totally indifferent, because he's the legitimate son. Oh yes, he's got nothing but contempt for me, and for him,

Indicates the YOUNG BOY.

for that poor little thing – we're bastards, you see. You understand? Bastards.

Goes over to the MOTHER *and embraces her.*

And this poor mother, who is the common mother of us all, he refuses to acknowledge as his own, and turns up his nose at her, as if she were only the mother of us three bastards. Despicable!

She says all this very rapidly, in a state of extreme agitation, and when she arrives at the final 'despicable' – her voice having reached a crescendo on 'bastards' – she pronounces the word quietly, but almost spits it out.

MOTHER (*with profound anguish, to the* DIRECTOR). Oh, sir, for the sake of these two poor little creatures, I implore you . . .

She feels faint, begins to sway.

Oh, my God . . .

The FATHER *rushes to support her, along with almost all the* ACTORS, *who are bewildered and anxious.*

FATHER. A chair, for pity's sake – a chair for this poor widow!

THE ACTORS (*running up*). Is this for real? Is she really fainting?

DIRECTOR. Let's have a chair here, quickly!

One of the ACTORS *brings up a chair; the others crowd round, showing concern. The* MOTHER, *now seated, tries to prevent the* FATHER *from lifting up the veil that hides her face.*

FATHER. Look at her, sir, look at her . . .

MOTHER. No, for God's sake – stop!

FATHER. Yes, let them see! (*He lifts up her veil.*)

MOTHER (*stands up and covers her face with her hands in sheer desperation*). Oh sir, I beg you – don't let this man do what he says, it's horrible!

DIRECTOR (*taken aback, dumbfounded*). I don't understand this – what on earth's going on? (*To the* FATHER.) Is this lady your wife?

FATHER (*quickly*). Yes, sir – she's my wife!

DIRECTOR. So how come she's a widow, if you're still alive?

The bewildered ACTORS *burst out laughing, in a sudden release of tension.*

FATHER (*offended, bitterly resentful*). Don't laugh! For God's sake, it's not funny! That's the whole point, sir, that's her drama. She had another man. Another man who ought to be here!

MOTHER (*shrieks*). No! No!

STEPDAUGHTER. He's dead, and well out of it. Two months ago, I've already said. And we're still in mourning, as you can see.

FATHER. Anyway, he's not here, and it's not because he's dead. He's not here because – well, just look at her, sir, and you'll soon understand! This isn't a drama about her love for two men, because she's frankly not capable of love – she couldn't feel anything, except maybe a little gratitude (not to me, of course – to him!) She's not a woman, she's a mother! And her drama (and it's powerful, sir, extremely powerful!) is in fact focused entirely on these four children, by the two men she's had.

MOTHER. I had them? You have the cheek to say I had them, as if that was what I wanted. No, sir, it was him! He forced me to go with that other man. He made me do it, he made me run away with him!

STEPDAUGHTER (*suddenly, indignant*). That's not true!

MOTHER (*astonished*). What d'you mean, it's not true?

STEPDAUGHTER. It's not true! It isn't!

MOTHER. How would you know?

STEPDAUGHTER. It's not true! (*To the* DIRECTOR.) Don't you believe it. D'you know why she says that? It's because of him, that's why! (*Indicating the* SON.) It's because she keeps tormenting herself, agonizing over that cold fish of a son of hers – yes, she wants him to believe that when she abandoned him at the age of two, it was because of him – (*Indicating the* FATHER.) it was because he forced her!

MOTHER (*vehemently*). He did force me, he did! As God is my witness! (*To the* DIRECTOR.) Ask him yourself if it isn't true! (*Indicating the* FATHER.) Make him admit it. (*Indicating the* STEPDAUGHTER.) She knows nothing about it.

STEPDAUGHTER. I know this much – while my father was alive, you were happy and contented, always. You can't deny that!

MOTHER. No, I can't deny it . . .

STEPDAUGHTER. He showed you nothing but love and kindness! (*To the* YOUNG BOY, *angrily.*) Isn't that the truth? Come on, speak up – why don't you say something, you idiot?

MOTHER. Oh, leave the poor boy alone! Why d'you want to make me appear ungrateful? I wouldn't dream of hurting your father. I'm just making the point that I wasn't to blame, nor did I take any pleasure in it, when I walked out on him and abandoned my son!

FATHER. That's true, sir. It was my fault.

A pause.

LEADING MAN (*to the other* ACTORS). This is some show!

LEADING LADY. And they're putting it on for us, now!

JUVENILE LEAD. Makes a change!

DIRECTOR (*beginning to be genuinely interested*). Let's listen to them! Listen, everybody!

Goes down one of the little staircases and stands in front of the stage, as if to get an audience's view of the scene.

SON (*without moving, quietly, in a cold, ironic manner*). Oh yes, let's listen to this philosophical gem. He's going to tell us all about his driving force − his 'mania for experiment'.

FATHER. You're a cynical fool! I've told you that a hundred times. (*To the* DIRECTOR, *now in the auditorium.*) He despises me, sir, because I've found these words to explain myself.

SON (*contemptuously*). Huh − words! That's such a consolation, isn't it, when we're faced by some event we can't explain, or some pain that's devouring us, and we find a word that basically means nothing, just gives us peace of mind!

STEPDAUGHTER. Yes, works a treat on remorse!

FATHER. Remorse? That's not true. It took more than words to do that, I can tell you.

STEPDAUGHTER. Oh, and a little bit of money, too – just a little. Like the hundred lire he was going to offer for my services, gentlemen!

The ACTORS *are horrified.*

SON (*with contempt for the* STEPDAUGHTER). That's disgusting!

STEPDAUGHTER. Disgusting? Well, it was there all right, in a pale blue envelope, lying on the little mahogany table in Madame Pace's back-shop. You know the set-up. One of those 'Madames' who sell *Robes et Manteaux* as a front to draw in girls like us, from good families, but with no money.

SON. And she thinks she's bought the right to tyrannize the whole lot of us, with that hundred lire he was going to pay for her, and which, as it turned out – now, note this down – he had no reason to pay.

STEPDAUGHTER. Ah yes, but we came pretty close, even so! (*Bursts out laughing.*)

MOTHER (*rising in protest*). Shame on you, daughter! Shame!

STEPDAUGHTER (*blurting out*). Shame? No, this is my revenge! I'm desperate to live out that scene, sirs – trembling with excitement! The room . . . here, a glass case, with a display of capes; over there, a sofa-bed; the mirror and a screen here; and in front of the window, the little mahogany table with the pale-blue envelope and the hundred lire. I see it so clearly! I could even pick it up.

You gentlemen really ought to turn your backs now – I'm almost naked! But I'm not blushing any longer – no, he's the one who's blushing! (*Indicates the* FATHER.) Though I can assure you he was quite pale, yes indeed, extremely pale, at that particular moment! (*To the* DIRECTOR.) Believe me, sir!

DIRECTOR. I'm losing track of this.

FATHER. No wonder! An outburst like that! Let's have a bit of order here, let me have my say, and don't listen to this disgraceful accusation, which this woman's so determined to lay on me, without giving me a chance to explain.

STEPDAUGHTER. Forget it! We don't want any of your tall stories here.

FATHER. What stories? I just want to explain a few things.

STEPDAUGHTER. Oh yes, I bet you do – in your own way, of course!

At this point the DIRECTOR *comes back up onto the stage in an attempt to take control.*

FATHER. I mean, isn't that where the trouble lies? In the words? We all have a world of things within us – each of us has his own private world. And how can we possibly understand one another, sir, if I invest the words I speak with the meaning and value that things have for me, in my private world, while the person listening to me inevitably receives them in accordance with the meaning and value they have for *him*, in his own private world? We think we understand each other, but we don't, ever! Just look – all my pity, the pity I felt for this woman

(*Indicates the* MOTHER.) . . . she chooses to interpret as the most savage cruelty!

MOTHER. But you threw me out of the house!

FATHER. D'you hear that? Threw her out! She honestly thinks I threw her out!

MOTHER. You know how to talk, and I don't . . . But believe me, sir – after he married me . . . God knows why! I was just a poor, simple woman . . .

FATHER. But that was precisely why – it was your simplicity I loved, that's why I married you, believing that . . .

Stops short as she is about to contradict him; flings his arms wide in a gesture of despair, seeing the impossibility of making her understand him, then turns to the DIRECTOR.

You see? She says no! It's frightening, sir, believe me, it's truly frightening, her deafness, her mental deafness! (*Taps his forehead.*) She's all heart, when it comes to her children, but as far as the brain's concerned, she's stone deaf, sir, to the point of desperation!

STEPDAUGHTER. Yes, well, just make him tell you what good *his* brains have done for us!

FATHER. If we could only foresee the harm that can come from the good we think we're doing!

At this point the LEADING LADY, *increasingly perturbed at the way the* LEADING MAN *is flirting with the* STEP-DAUGHTER, *comes downstage to speak to the* DIRECTOR.

LEADING LADY. Excuse me, sir – are we continuing with this rehearsal or not?

DIRECTOR. Yes, yes, of course. But let me hear this first.

JUVENILE LEAD. This is a really novel idea!

INGENUE. It's absolutely fascinating!

LEADING LADY. If you're *that* easily fascinated! (*Looking daggers at the* LEADING MAN.)

DIRECTOR (*to the* FATHER). However, you will need to explain yourself more clearly. (*Sits down.*)

FATHER. All right. Well, sir, the thing is – I had this poor fellow working for me, my assistant – secretary, really – absolutely devoted. And he had a wonderful understanding with my wife here. (*Indicates the* MOTHER.) No suggestion of wrongdoing – heaven forbid! He was a good, simple person like herself, and not only were they both incapable of doing wrong, the thought would never even have entered their minds!

STEPDAUGHTER. Yes, the thought entered *his* mind instead, so he did it for them!

FATHER. That's not true! I only wanted to do what was best for them – and for myself too, yes, I admit it! Sir, there came a point when I couldn't say one word to either of them, without a knowing look passing between them. One would suddenly try and catch the other's eye, for some hint about how to react to what I'd just said, so as not to make me angry. Well, that was enough, as I'm sure you'll understand, to keep me constantly in a foul mood – it was so exasperating, I couldn't bear it.

DIRECTOR. I'm sorry, but why didn't you just sack him, this secretary of yours?

FATHER. Exactly, yes! I *did* sack him. But then I had to watch this poor woman hanging around the house like a lost soul – like some sort of stray dog that you would take in out of pity.

MOTHER. And no wonder!

FATHER (*hastily, turning as if to forestall her*). It's about our son, isn't it?

MOTHER. The first thing he did, sir – he snatched my son away from me!

FATHER. But not from cruelty! It was so he would grow up strong and healthy, in touch with the soil.

STEPDAUGHTER (*indicating the* SON, *mockingly*). Yes, and just look at him!

FATHER (*quickly*). So that's my fault too, is it, that he's turned out like this? Sir, I sent him to a wet nurse in the country, a peasant woman, because I didn't think she was strong enough, even though she was from humble origins herself. In fact, that was the reason I'd married her. It sounds silly, I know, but what else could I do? I've always had this damnable yearning for a certain kind of sound moral health.

At this point, the STEPDAUGHTER *again bursts out into raucous laughter.*

Oh, make her stop that – this is intolerable!

DIRECTOR. Stop it, for heaven's sake! Let me listen!

At the DIRECTOR's *rebuke, she suddenly stops laughing, in mid-guffaw, and becomes abstracted and withdrawn, a half-smile*

on her lips. The DIRECTOR *descends into the auditorium once
again to see how the stage looks.*

FATHER. I couldn't bear the sight of this woman any
longer. (*Indicates the* MOTHER.) And it wasn't so much
the way she annoyed me, or frankly suffocated me, but
the compassion I had for her, the genuine anguish I felt
on her behalf.

MOTHER. And he sent me away!

FATHER. Well provided for, sir – to that man, to free her
from me!

MOTHER. And to free himself!

FATHER. Myself too, sir, yes – I admit it. All right, it went
badly wrong. But I did it with the best of intentions –
more for her sake than mine, I swear it!

Folds his arms across his chest, then suddenly turns to the
MOTHER.

And I didn't ever lose sight of you, did I. No, you were
never out of my sight until that man carried you off one
day without my knowledge, to another town, because he'd
stupidly misinterpreted my innocent concern for you –
that's right, sir, innocent, no ulterior motive whatsoever.
My interest in this new little family, as it grew up, was
incredibly affectionate. As she can confirm! (*Indicates the*
STEPDAUGHTER.)

STEPDAUGHTER. I can indeed! Well, I was such a sweet
little thing, wasn't I. Pigtails over my shoulders, knickers
hanging down under my skirt – a right little sweetheart.
And he'd be outside the school watching for me. Come
to see how I was maturing . . .

FATHER. That's disgusting! Shame on you!

STEPDAUGHTER. No? Then why?

FATHER. Absolutely shameful!

In his agitation, turns quickly to the DIRECTOR *to explain.*

Sir, after she went away (*Indicating the* MOTHER.), the
house suddenly seemed so empty. She was a nightmare,
yes, but she filled the whole place. And left all alone,
I found myself wandering through those rooms like a lost
soul. This lad here (*Indicating the* SON.) was brought up
apart from me, and when he did come back home, well,
I don't know – he didn't seem mine any longer. What
was missing between us was the mother, so he grew up
on his own, by himself, having no real contact with me,
either emotional or intellectual. And then (it sounds
strange, sir, but it's what happened), very gradually – at
first through curiosity – I became attracted to this little
family of hers, which I had brought into being. The
thought of it began to fill the void which I felt all around
me. I had a need, a genuine need to believe that she
was at peace now, wholly wrapped up in the simple cares
of life, enjoying her good fortune well away from my
complicated spiritual agonies. And to prove it, I used to
go and watch that little girl coming out of school.

STEPDAUGHTER. Oh, yes! He'd follow me down the
street, he'd smile at me, and when I got to the house
he'd wave – like this! And I'd give him a dirty look,
suspicious – I mean, I'd no idea who he was! I told
my mother, and of course she knew immediately. (*The*
MOTHER *nods in agreement.*) At first she wouldn't send
me back to school – that went on for days. And when

I did go back, I saw him again at the school gate – sort
of funny-looking, holding a big brown-paper bag. He
came over and gave me a cuddle, then took an enormous
straw hat out of the bag – really beautiful, with tiny little
May roses all round the brim – and it was for me!

DIRECTOR. This isn't drama, this is narrative.

SON (*scornfully*). Of course it is – it's literature.

FATHER. What d'you mean, literature? This is life, sir!
Passion!

DIRECTOR. That's as may be. But it can't be staged.

FATHER. Yes, yes, I agree. This is all background material.
I'm not saying it should be staged. I mean, for a start
(*Indicates the* STEPDAUGHTER.), she's no longer that
little girl with the pigtails over her shoulder . . .

STEPDAUGHTER. Or her knickers hanging down!

FATHER. Anyway, the drama begins now, sir. Fresh, and
complicated.

STEPDAUGHTER (*steps forward, proud and melancholy*). Soon
after my father died . . .

FATHER (*hastily, cutting her off*). Extreme poverty, sir! So they
came back here, and I knew nothing about it. Thanks
to her pigheadedness! (*Indicates the* MOTHER.) She can
barely write, but she could've got her daughter, or the
boy, to let me know they needed help.

MOTHER. Now tell me, sir, how was I to know what he
was feeling?

FATHER. That's been your mistake all long – you never
had the least idea of my feelings!

MOTHER. Well, having been apart so many years, and after all that had happened . . .

FATHER. Yes, and is it my fault that that man spirited you away like that? (*Turning to the* DIRECTOR.) I mean, practically overnight – he got himself another job some place, miles away. I couldn't possibly find them, so inevitably over the years my interest in them faded. But the drama exploded, sir, violently and unexpectedly, on their return. When I was driven, sad to say, by the shameful needs of the flesh. It's sheer misery, truly it is, for a man on his own, who has no taste for sordid liaisons; when he's not old enough to do without women, but not young enough to go casually looking for one without shame. Misery? Was that what I said? It's horror – pure horror! Because no woman can give him love any more. And when you realise this, well, you should just give up. Oh, yes! Outwardly, in front of other people, we all put on a certain kind of dignity, but inwardly, we're well aware of the unspeakable things that pass through our minds. And we give in, we yield to temptation, only to bounce back up again immediately, eager to restore that dignity of ours, solid and intact, like a headstone above a grave, burying every last trace and memory of our shame, hiding it even from our own eyes. Everybody does it! They don't all have the courage to admit it, though.

STEPDAUGHTER. Yes, but you've all got the courage to do it!

FATHER. That's right. But only in secret. So it actually takes more courage to say it. I mean, you've only got to say these things, and behold – you're labelled a cynic!

But it's not true, sir – we're just like everybody else,
perhaps even better, because we're not afraid to shine the
light of our intelligence on the dark red shame of man's
bestial nature, which other people close their eyes to.
A woman, for example – what does she do? She gazes
at you invitingly, egging you on. So you take hold of her,
and she's no sooner in your arms than she closes her
eyes. It's the sign of her submission, the sign that says
to a man: 'Be blind, for I am blind!'

STEPDAUGHTER. And when she stops closing her eyes?
When she no longer feels the need to close her eyes to
her own dark red shame, but dry-eyed and unmoved,
looks on his shame instead, the shame of a man who can
blind himself without even love? Oh, it makes me sick,
it really does – all this sophistry, all this logic-chopping
to prove man's bestial nature, and then justify it, make
excuses for it! I can't bear to listen! I mean, when you're
compelled to 'simplify' life in that way, reducing it to the
level of the beasts, casting aside everything that makes us
human, every chaste desire, every pure feeling – our
sense of idealism, duty, modesty, shame – well, there's
nothing more contemptible and nauseating than that kind
of remorse – crocodile tears!

DIRECTOR. Look, can we get to the point? Can we get to
the action? This is all talk.

FATHER. Yes, of course, sir. But action's like a sack – it
won't stand up if it's empty. And to make it stand up,
you first need to fill it with all the reasons and feelings
that have brought it about. I mean, after that man died,
and they came back here in abject poverty, how could I
possibly have known that she (*Indicating the* MOTHER.) –

in order to support her family – would take a job as a
seamstress, and with Madame Pace of all people!

STEPDAUGHTER. Who is a first-class dressmaker, if you
must know! On the surface, she serves the finest society
ladies, but she has things neatly arranged so that they in
fact serve her, as a front for her other activities!

MOTHER. Sir, you must believe me – I hadn't the faintest
suspicion. It never once entered my mind that that old
hag only took me on because she had her eye on my
daughter.

STEPDAUGHTER. Poor Mamma! D'you know what that
woman would do, sir, when I took back the work my
mother had done? She'd show me how my mother had
ruined the dress she'd given her to sew – and she'd
deduct it from my wages, so I ended up having to pay
her. And all the time this poor woman imagined she was
making sacrifices for me and those two, sitting up half
the night sewing dresses for Madame Pace!

The ACTORS *register their disgust.*

DIRECTOR (*quickly*). And one day, in that very place, you
encountered . . .

STEPDAUGHTER (*indicating the* FATHER). Him! Yes, sir –
him! One of her regulars. What a scene that'll be!
Wonderful!

FATHER. With her, the mother, arriving . . .

STEPDAUGHTER (*quickly, spitefully*). Almost in time!

FATHER (*shouting*). No, just in time! Just in time! Because
fortunately I realised who she was, just in time! And

I took them all back home with me, sir. But you can imagine how things are between us now, given the way she is, and the fact I can't even look her in the eye!

STEPDAUGHTER. This is ridiculous! I mean, how could I possibly now claim to be a modest little miss, well brought up and virtuous, in line with his damned pretensions to 'sound moral health'?

FATHER. But that's the whole essence of the drama, sir, as I see it – the fact that we each think of ourselves as one person, but it's not true. We're all so many different people, sir, as many as we have the potential to be. We're one thing with one person, and something quite different with another! Meanwhile we labour under the illusion that we're the same with everybody, and that we're the same in everything we do. Well, that's not so – it's simply not true. And we're made painfully aware of this when by sheer misfortune, in the course of some act or other, we're suddenly pulled up short and left dangling in mid-air. What I mean is that we're aware of not being totally involved in that act, so it's terribly unfair to judge us by that alone – to keep us dangling there, pilloried, as it were, for the rest of our lives, summed up by that one single event! Now do you understand this girl's treachery? She caught me quite by accident, in a place I shouldn't have been, doing something she shouldn't have known about – and now she wants to impose a kind of reality on me, one that I wouldn't have dreamed of assuming for her, in that shameful, fleeting instant in my life! That's what really pains me, sir. But you can see the kind of power it'll bring to the drama. And then there's the situation of the others – his, for instance . . . (*Indicates the* SON.)

SON (*with a contemptuous shrug*). You can leave me out of it, it's nothing to do with me.

FATHER. What d'you mean, nothing to do with you?

SON. I don't come into this, and I don't want to. You know perfectly well I wasn't meant to be involved with you people.

STEPDAUGHTER. Oh no, we're just the common herd, and he's so refined! But you must have noticed, sir, how often I give him a look of utter contempt, and he has to lower his eyes – that's because he knows how much harm he's done me.

SON (*without looking at her*). Who, me?

STEPDAUGHTER. Yes, you! It's because of you, my darling, that I'm on the streets!

The ACTORS *are horrified.*

Tell us, yes or no – didn't you, with that attitude of yours – didn't you deny us . . . well, I won't say the intimacy of your home, but even the sort of basic hospitality that makes a guest feel at ease? No, we were intruders, coming to invade your kingdom, your precious 'legitimacy'! Really, sir, I just wish you had a private view of certain little scenes between him and me. I mean, he says I tyrannized over them all. But don't you see? It was precisely that attitude of his that drove me to exploit the situation – he calls it a cheap trick – through which I came into his home with my mother, who also happens to be *his* mother – and took charge of it!

SON (*slowly coming forward*). They're really having fun, aren't they – it's too easy, the whole lot of them, ganging up against me. But you just imagine you're somebody's son, sitting peacefully at home, and one fine day a young woman just walks in, bold as brass, looks down her nose at you, and demands to see your father – to discuss God only knows what. Later on she comes back, nose in the air still, and this time she's accompanied by that little creature there. And finally she addresses your father – God knows why – in the most cryptic and offhand manner, asking him for money in a tone of voice that implies he's got to give her it, because he's absolutely obliged to –

FATHER. But I *am* obliged to, that's the point – it's for your mother!

SON. My mother? So how was I to know that? I mean, when I've never once set eyes on her? (*To the* DIRECTOR.) Never once heard her spoken about? She just shows up one day with her (*Indicating the* STEPDAUGHTER.), and that boy, and the little girl, and they say to me, 'Oh, didn't you know? This is *your* mother too!' And eventually I manage to figure out, from her manner (*Points again to the* STEPDAUGHTER.), just why they'd suddenly taken up residence in our house. What I'm going through, what I'm feeling, sir, I can't express and I've no desire to. I don't even want to think about it. So, obviously, I can't take any part in this action. You've got to believe me, sir – I'm not a fully-realised character, dramatically speaking, and I feel extremely ill at ease in their company, so please leave me out of it!

FATHER. What? No, I'm sorry, but it's precisely because you're so –

SON (*violently exasperated*). Because I'm so what? How would you know? When have you ever given a damn about me?

FATHER. All right, all right – point taken. But isn't that still a dramatic situation? This distancing of yourself, from your mother and me, it's so cruel – I mean, she comes back home, sees you virtually for the first time, a grown man – she doesn't even recognise you, all she knows is that you're her very own son . . . (*Drawing the* DIRECTOR*'s attention to the* MOTHER.) Look, sir, look – she's weeping!

STEPDAUGHTER (*in a fury, stamping her foot*). Yes, like an idiot!

FATHER (*drawing the* DIRECTOR*'s attention to the* STEPDAUGHTER *also*). And she can't abide him, you know. (*Turning again to the* SON.) He says it's nothing to do with him, but he's virtually the pivot of the action. Look at that young lad there, clinging onto his mother – frightened, humiliated . . . And he's like that because of *him!* His is possibly the most painful situation of all – he feels alienated, more so than the rest. Poor little thing, he's quite mortified, he's distraught at being taken into our home, out of charity, as it were . . . (*Confidentially.*) He's just like his father – meek and mild, never speaks . . .

DIRECTOR. Even so, it's not a good idea, having him. Children are nothing but trouble on stage, believe me.

FATHER. But he wouldn't be any trouble, at least not for long. Nor would the little girl – I mean, she's the first to go.

DIRECTOR. Splendid, yes! I must say this intrigues me, I find it all extremely interesting. I have a distinct feeling there's a good play to be dug out of this material.

STEPDAUGHTER (*trying to interpose herself*). Yes, with a character like me in it!

FATHER (*pushing her aside, anxious to learn the* DIRECTOR's *decision*). You keep out of it!

DIRECTOR (*continuing, ignoring the interruption*). Yes, this is something new . . .

FATHER. Oh, absolutely new, sir!

DIRECTOR. It takes some nerve, though, I must say – to walk in and fling all this at me . . .

FATHER. Well, sir – people like us, you see, born to the stage . . .

DIRECTOR. You're amateur actors?

FATHER. No no – I say 'born to the stage' because we're . . .

DIRECTOR. Oh, come on – you must have done some acting!

FATHER. No, not at all, sir. Only insofar as each of us acts out a part in life – one that's been assigned to him by himself or by other people. And as you see in my case, passion can run a little high at times – the way it does in all of us – and become rather stagy . . .

DIRECTOR. Well, we'll let that pass. But you do understand, my dear sir, that without an author . . . I mean, I could put you in touch with someone who . . .

FATHER. No, no, please – you be the author!

DIRECTOR. Me? What are you talking about?

FATHER. You, sir – yes, you. Why not?

DIRECTOR. But I've never written a play in my life!

FATHER. So? Now's the time to make a start. There's nothing to it. Everybody's doing it. And your job'll be a lot easier having us all here, alive and kicking, right in front of you.

DIRECTOR. But that's not enough.

FATHER. What d'you mean, not enough? Seeing us live out our own drama . . . ?

DIRECTOR. That's as may be, but you still need somebody who can write it.

FATHER. No, sir – somebody to *transcribe* it, possibly, but he'll have it all here in front of him, live, scene by scene. All we need at this point is some sort of rough sketch, and then you can start rehearsing.

DIRECTOR (*intrigued, goes back up on stage*). Hm . . . yes . . . I'm tempted . . . Might be fun . . . I suppose we could give it a try . . .

FATHER. Of course you could! Just wait till you see the kind of scenes that come out of it! I can list them for you right now!

DIRECTOR. Yes . . . I'm quite tempted . . . Let's give it a try. We'll go along to my office. (*Turning to the* ACTORS.) You can take a break now, but don't go too far away. Back here in fifteen or twenty minutes. (*To the* FATHER.)

Now, let's try this out. We just might get something extraordinary out of this.

FATHER. Oh, for sure, sir! But wouldn't it be better if they
came too? (*Indicating the other* CHARACTERS.)

DIRECTOR. Yes, yes – let them come! (*Makes to exit, then
turns back to address the* ACTORS *again.*) Now, don't forget.
Back on time – quarter of an hour!

The DIRECTOR *and the* SIX CHARACTERS *cross the
stage and go out. The* ACTORS *remain, looking at one another,
astonished.*

LEADING MAN. He can't be serious. What's he trying to
do?

JUVENILE LEAD. This is absolutely crazy.

THIRD ACTOR. We're supposed to improvise a play, just
off the top of our heads?

JUVENILE LEAD. Yes, like the Commedia dell'Arte.

LEADING LADY. Well, if he thinks I'm getting mixed up
in that sort of nonsense . . .

INGENUE. Me neither – you can count me out!

FOURTH ACTOR. Who are these people? That's what I'd
like to know.

THIRD ACTOR. Who do you think? They're either
lunatics or crooks!

JUVENILE LEAD. And he's giving them a hearing?

INGENUE. It's sheer vanity – he fancies himself as an
author . . .

LEADING MAN. This is absolutely unheard of! I tell you, my friends, if this is what the theatre's coming to . . .

FIFTH ACTOR. Actually, I think it's quite amusing.

THIRD ACTOR. Huh! Well, we'll see. Let's just see what comes out of this.

The ACTORS *continue to talk amongst themselves as they leave the stage, some going out through the upstage door, others back to their dressing-rooms. The curtain remains up, and there is an interval of twenty minutes.*

The theatre warning bell is rung to announce the resumption of the play.

The ACTORS, STAGE MANAGER, TECHNICIAN, PROMPTER *and* PROPS MAN *make their way back to the stage from the dressing-rooms, door, and auditorium, at the same time as the* DIRECTOR *returns from his office with the* SIX CHARACTERS.

When the house lights are extinguished, the stage lighting is as before.

DIRECTOR. Now, let's go, everybody! Are we all here? Come on now, pay attention – let's get started! Where's the technician?

TECHNICIAN. I'm here!

DIRECTOR. Right, we want the stage set for the parlour scene – two flats and a drop with a door in it'll do – quickly, please.

The TECHNICIAN *speedily sets to work, and while the* DIRECTOR *carries on talking about the play with the* STAGE MANAGER, PROPS MAN, PROMPTER, *and* ACTORS,

*the required setting is assembled: two wing flats and a backdrop
with a pink and gold-striped door.*

DIRECTOR (*to the* PROPS MAN). Go and see if you can
find a divan in the props room.

PROPS MAN. Right, sir – there's a green one.

DIRECTOR. No no, not green. There used to be a yellow
floral one, an enormous thing, plush velvet – very
comfortable.

PROPS MAN. No, we haven't got one like that.

DIRECTOR. Well, it doesn't matter. Use whatever's there.

STEPDAUGHTER. What d'you mean, it doesn't matter?
Madame Pace's famous chaise-longue?

DIRECTOR. This is just a run-through. Please, don't
interfere! (*To the* STAGE MANAGER.) See if you can get
hold of a glass case – preferably quite long and low.

STEPDAUGHTER. And the table, the little mahogany
table for the blue envelope!

STAGE MANAGER (*to the* DIRECTOR). Well, there's that
little gilt one.

DIRECTOR. Fine, that'll do.

FATHER. And a mirror.

STEPDAUGHTER. And the screen! Don't forget the screen
– I can't manage without it!

STAGE MANAGER. That's all right, miss. We've got
plenty of screens, don't worry.

DIRECTOR (*to the* STEPDAUGHTER). And we need some coat-racks and suchlike, don't we?

STEPDAUGHTER. Oh yes – lots!

DIRECTOR (*to the* STAGE MANAGER). See what we've got, and bring them up.

STAGE MANAGER. Right, sir – I'll do that.

The STAGE MANAGER *hurries off to fulfil his task, and while the* DIRECTOR *speaks with the* PROMPTER, *and later the* CHARACTERS *and* ACTORS, *the furniture is brought on by* STAGEHANDS, *and placed on the stage as the* STAGE MANAGER *directs.*

DIRECTOR (*to the* PROMPTER). Right, you can get into position now. Here – this is an outline of the play, act by act. (*Hands him a few sheets of paper.*) You'll have to work miracles today.

PROMPTER. Shorthand?

DIRECTOR (*pleasantly surprised*). Splendid! You can do shorthand?

PROMPTER. Well, I may not be much of a prompter, but when it comes to shorthand . . .

DIRECTOR. That's better still! (*Turning to a* STAGEHAND.) Go and get some paper from my office – lots of it, as much you can find.

The STAGEHAND *hurries out and quickly returns with a sizeable wad of paper, which he hands to the* PROMPTER.

DIRECTOR (*continuing to the* PROMPTER). Now, just follow the scenes as we play them, and try to get the dialogue down – at least the more important stuff. (*Then, turning to the* ACTORS.) Right, ladies and gentlemen, clear the stage, please! Everybody over here (*Indicates stage left.*), and pay close attention.

LEADING LADY. Excuse me, but we . . .

DIRECTOR (*cutting her off*). Don't worry, nobody's asking you to improvise!

LEADING MAN. So what are we supposed to be doing?

DIRECTOR. Nothing! Just listen and watch for the moment. You'll all have a proper script later – this is simply a run-through, as best we can. They're going to do it. (*Indicates the* CHARACTERS.)

FATHER (*as if suddenly awakened from a trance, amid the on-stage confusion*). Us? I'm sorry, but what d'you mean by a run-through?

DIRECTOR. A try-out. A rehearsal for them. (*Indicates the* ACTORS.)

FATHER. But if we already *are* the characters . . .

DIRECTOR. Yes, yes, of course you're the characters. But characters don't act here, my dear sir. It's actors who do the acting. The characters stay there in the script . . . (*Indicates the* PROMPTER's *box.*) That's when there *is* a script!

FATHER. But that's the whole point! Since there isn't one, and you people are lucky enough to have the characters standing here in front of you . . .

DIRECTOR. Oh, wonderful! So now you want to do it all yourselves? To act, to appear before the public?

FATHER. Yes, absolutely – just the way we are.

DIRECTOR. Huh! That'll be some performance, I can assure you!

LEADING MAN. So what are we standing around here for, then?

DIRECTOR. You surely don't imagine you can act, do you? Don't make me laugh! (*The* ACTORS *actually do laugh.*) You see, they *are* laughing! Anyway – back to business. We need to cast the play. That's easy enough – they virtually cast themselves. (*To the* SECOND ACTRESS.) You, my dear, will play the Mother. (*To the* FATHER.) We'll need to find a name for her.

FATHER. Amalia, sir.

DIRECTOR. But that's your wife's name. We don't want to call her by her real name!

FATHER. I'm sorry, but why not? I mean, if that's what she's called . . . Well, I suppose if this lady's going to play the part . . . (*Gestures vaguely in the direction of the* SECOND ACTRESS). Actually, I see *this* woman as Amalia, sir. (*Indicates the* MOTHER.) But it's up to you. (*Becoming ever more confused.*) I don't know what to say now . . . I'm starting to . . . oh, I don't know – it's as if I'm hearing my own words as false, somehow – they don't ring true.

DIRECTOR. Oh, don't worry about that – don't give it a second thought. Leave all that to us – we'll find the right tone. As for the name – well, if you want 'Amalia', then Amalia it shall be. Or we can find something else. Anyway, for the moment, we'll dispense with names. (*To the* JUVENILE LEAD.) You, sir, are the Son. (*To the*

LEADING LADY.) And you, dear lady, are obviously the Stepdaughter.

STEPDAUGHTER (*animatedly*). What? What did you say? That woman there is *me*? (*Bursts out laughing.*)

DIRECTOR (*angrily*). What's so funny?

LEADING LADY (*indignant*). No-one has ever *dared* laugh at me! I demand some respect, otherwise I'm going right now!

STEPDAUGHTER. No no, I'm sorry – I'm not laughing at you.

DIRECTOR (*to the* STEPDAUGHTER). You should feel privileged to be played by . . .

LEADING LADY (*breaks in, contemptuously*). 'That woman there'!

STEPDAUGHTER. I didn't mean you, honestly. I was thinking about myself, because I just can't see anything of myself in you, that's all. I don't know, really . . . I mean, you're not in the least like me!

FATHER. That's right, sir. You see, what we're trying to express . . .

DIRECTOR. What d'you mean, express? D'you think it's all there inside you, just waiting to come out? Not a chance!

FATHER. What? We're not capable of expressing ourselves?

DIRECTOR. Absolutely not! What you're trying to express simply becomes raw material here, to which the actors give body and form, speech and gesture. And for your information, sir, these actors have managed to give expression to far greater material than yours. Yours is so trivial, that if it should work at all on stage, the credit, you can believe me, will be entirely due to my actors.

FATHER. I wouldn't dream of arguing with you, sir, but this is an extremely painful business for us, who are as you see us, with these bodies, with these faces . . .

DIRECTOR (*cutting him off, impatiently*). Oh, we can fix all that with make-up. Make-up'll do the trick, my dear sir, as far as looks are concerned.

FATHER. Yes, but the voice, the gestures . . .

DIRECTOR. Oh, for heaven's sake, you can't exist as your real self here! An actor'll play you, and there's an end to it.

FATHER. Yes, I understand, sir. But I think I'm beginning to see why our author, who actually saw us alive, the way we are now, didn't want to put us on stage. I don't want to offend your actors, sir – God forbid! But when I think of watching myself being played by . . . well, who knows? . . .

The LEADING MAN *rises imperiously and walks over to confront the* FATHER, *followed by some* YOUNG ACTRESSES, *laughing.*

LEADING MAN. By me, if you've no objections!

FATHER (*ingratiatingly*). I'm deeply honoured, sir. (*Bows.*) Even so, I still think that, with the best will in the world, and all his professional skill, no matter how hard this gentleman tries to identify with me . . . (*Stops short, confused.*)

LEADING MAN. Go on, spit it out! (*The* ACTRESSES *laugh.*)

FATHER. Well . . . what I mean is that the performance
he'll give, even if he *is* made up to look like me . . . well,
for a start – with his height . . . (*All the* ACTORS *laugh.*)
I mean, it'll be extremely difficult to portray me as I truly
am. It'll be more like – all right, leaving aside the face –
it'll be more like his interpretation of me, how he feels
like me – that's if he *does* feel like me – rather than how
I actually feel within myself. And it seems to me that
anybody who's called upon to judge us, ought to take
that into account.

DIRECTOR. So you're already worried about the critics?
And I'm still waiting to make a start! Well, let the critics
say what they like – we need to concentrate on putting
on this play – *if* we can! (*Moves a little way apart, and looks
around.*) Right, let's go! Is the set ready? (*To the* ACTORS
and CHARACTERS.) Move back a bit, let's have a look.
(*Climbs down from the stage.*) We can't waste any more time.
(*To the* STEPDAUGHTER.) How's the set look to you –
all right?

STEPDAUGHTER. Mm . . . To be honest, no – I don't
recognise it.

DIRECTOR. Oh, for heaven's sake, we can't reconstruct
Madame Pace's back room on stage, you know! (*To the
FATHER.*) You said it was a parlour, with floral
wallpaper?

FATHER. That's right, sir – white.

DIRECTOR. Well, it's not white, it's striped, but that
doesn't matter. And we're more or less there with the
furniture, I think. That little table – move that a bit
further downstage. (*A* STAGEHAND *does so.*) (*To the*

PROPS MAN.) Find an envelope meantime, pale blue
if possible, and give it to this gentleman. (*Indicates the*
FATHER.)

PROPS MAN. An ordinary letter envelope?

DIRECTOR AND FATHER. Yes, yes, for a letter.

PROPS MAN. Right! (*Goes out.*)

DIRECTOR. Now, let's go! The young lady's on first. (*The*
LEADING LADY *moves into centre stage.*) No no, not you.
I was speaking to the young lady. (*Meaning the*
STEPDAUGHTER.) You stay there and watch . . .

STEPDAUGHTER (*quickly interjecting*) . . . How I live it!

LEADING LADY (*offended*). I'll live it too, don't you worry,
once I get into it!

DIRECTOR (*clutching his head*). Ladies, ladies, no more chit-
chat, please! Right, scene one – the Young Lady and
Madame Pace. Oh . . . (*Looks around, confused, and climbs
back up on stage.*) This Madame Pace person . . .

FATHER. She's not with us, sir.

DIRECTOR. So what do we do now?

FATHER. Well, she's alive – she's alive too!

DIRECTOR. Yes, I'm sure – but where?

FATHER. Hold on, I'll tell you. (*Turning to the*
ACTRESSES.) If you ladies would be so kind as to let
me have your hats a moment . . .

ACTRESSES (*slightly surprised and amused, in chorus*). What?
Our hats? What does he want? What for? Good gracious!

DIRECTOR. What do you want with the ladies' hats? (*The* ACTORS *laugh.*)

FATHER. Oh, nothing – I'm just putting them on these stands for a bit. And if some of you would be so kind as to take off your coats as well . . .

ACTORS (*surprised and amused, in chorus*). Coats as well? What next? The man's mad!

ACTRESSES (*as before*). What for? Just the coat?

FATHER. Yes, just to hang up, for a minute or two. If you'd be so kind? All right?

The ACTRESSES, *continuing to laugh, take off their hats, and a few of them their coats also, and hang them up on the racks.*

ACTRESSES. Well, why not? There you are! This is getting quite funny. D'you want us to put them on display?

FATHER. Yes, that's it exactly, miss! As if they were on show.

DIRECTOR. Would you mind telling me what you're doing?

FATHER. Well, it's like this, sir – if we prepare the stage properly, she might be attracted by the tools of her trade, as it were. I mean, who knows? She might even appear amongst us . . .

He invites them all to look in the direction of the upstage door.

Look! Look!

The upstage door opens and MADAME PACE *takes a few steps forward. She is an enormously fat old harridan, heavily made up, and sporting an absurd carroty red wig, with a crimson rose over her ear, Spanish-style. She wears a gaudy, but elegant red silk dress, holds an ostrich-feather fan in one hand, and a cigarette upraised between two fingers in the other. At the sight of this apparition, the* ACTORS *and the* DIRECTOR *instantly cry out with fear and leap from the stage into the auditorium, heading for the aisles. The* STEPDAUGHTER, *by contrast, runs up to* MADAME PACE *submissively, as if to her mistress.*

STEPDAUGHTER. Here she is! She's here!

FATHER (*beaming*). It's her! Didn't I tell you? She's here!

DIRECTOR (*recovering from the shock, now indignant*). Is this some sort of trick?

LEADING MAN. What's the hell's going on here?

JUVENILE LEAD (*almost simultaneously*). A walk-on? Where did she spring from?

INGENUE (*as above*). They've been keeping her up their sleeve!

LEADING LADY (*as above*). It's a conjuring trick, that's what it is!

FATHER (*over the clamour*). Excuse me! Listen! Why do you want to spoil a miracle like this, for the sake of boring, commonplace truth? This is a miraculous reality which is born, called forth, attracted, given form by the stage itself, and which has more right to live here than you, because it's infinitely truer than you. Which of you actresses is going to play Madame Pace? Eh? Well, that's Madame Pace over there. And I'm sure you'll agree that the actress who plays her will be less true than this lady – that is, herself in person! Look – you see? My daughter has recognised her, and gone up immediately to greet her! Now – just watch this scene.

The DIRECTOR *and* ACTORS *hesitantly go back up on stage. Meanwhile, even during the protests, and the* FATHER's *response, the scene between the* STEPDAUGHTER *and* MADAME PACE *has already begun, played very quietly, almost in whispers – that is, naturally – in a way that would be impossible to stage. When the* ACTORS *are called to attention by the* FATHER, *they turn to watch* MADAME PACE *put her hand under the* STEPDAUGHTER's *chin, lifting up her head, and are intrigued for a moment, listening intently. However, since they can't hear what is being said, they soon lose interest.*

DIRECTOR. Well?

LEADING MAN. What's she saying?

LEADING LADY. You can't hear a thing!

JUVENILE LEAD. Louder! Louder!

STEPDAUGHTER (*leaving* MADAME PACE, *who is smiling enigmatically, and coming downstage to confront the* ACTORS). Louder? What d'you mean 'louder'? You can't say these kind of things out loud! All right, I could shout the odds at him (*Indicates the* FATHER.) a minute ago, but that was to shame him, that was for revenge! It's a very different matter for Madame Pace, sirs – she could go to jail!

DIRECTOR. Yes, that's all well and good, but you need to make yourself heard in the theatre, my dear. I mean, *we* can't even hear you, and we're up on stage! You imagine what it'll be like for an audience. You've got to put it across. Anyway, you certainly can speak out loud, between yourselves, since we won't be here listening, the way we

are now. Just pretend you're alone in the back shop, with
nobody to hear you.

The STEPDAUGHTER, *with a hint of malice in her smile,
wags an elegant finger several times, as if to say no.*

DIRECTOR. What d'you mean, 'no'?

STEPDAUGHTER (*in an undertone, mysteriously*). There *is*
someone who'll hear us, sir, if she (*Indicating* MADAME
PACE.) speaks out loud.

DIRECTOR (*dismayed*). Don't tell me you're going to
conjure up somebody else!

The ACTORS *make as if to leap from the stage again.*

FATHER. No no, sir. She's referring to me. I'm supposed to
be over there, waiting behind the door. And Madame
Pace knows this. So, with your permission, I'll go there
now, to be ready.

He makes to go upstage. The DIRECTOR *stops him.*

DIRECTOR. No, hold on, wait! We have to respect
the conventions of the theatre. Before you're ready to
enter . . .

STEPDAUGHTER (*interrupting him*). Let's get on with it!
Let's do it now! I'm desperate to do that scene, I am,
honestly. If he's ready to do it now, I'm ready and willing!

DIRECTOR (*shouting*). But we've got to play this scene first,
between you and her (*Indicating* MADAME PACE.) so it
can be heard! Do you understand?

STEPDAUGHTER. Oh, for God's sake, sir – she only told
me what you already know: Mamma's work's not up to

scratch again, the material's ruined, and I'll just have to put up with it, if I want her to keep helping us, the wretched state we're in.

MADAME PACE (*coming downstage with an air of great importance*). Si, signore – ees *perché io non voglio* make profit, take *vantaggio* – *ha capito?*

DIRECTOR (*alarmed*). Good God! Is that the way she speaks?

The ACTORS *all burst out laughing.*

STEPDAUGHTER (*also laughing*). Indeed she does, sir – a mixture of English and Italian, it's terribly funny.

MADAME PACE. Hey, ees *non educato* you laugh at me, *signore* – I speak Eengleesh *come meglio posso!*

DIRECTOR. No, no, that's fine. Speak like that – just carry on speaking like that, dear lady, that'll do nicely. Couldn't be better – a bit of humour to soften the harsh reality of the situation. Just carry on – that's splendid.

STEPDAUGHTER. Of course it is! I mean, you hear yourself being propositioned in that sort of language – well, it's perfect, it's like a great joke. You have to laugh, haven't you, when you hear there's a *vecchio signore* – an old gentleman – who would like to *divertirsi* – to have fun with you – isn't that so, Madame Pace?

MADAME PACE. No no, ees no *vecchio* – *ebbene*, maybe a leetle – *un po' vecchio, sì?* But ees better for you – maybe you no like, but ees *discreto, no?*

The MOTHER *leaps to her feet, to the astonishment and dismay of the* ACTORS, *who have taken no notice of her until now.*

They are startled when she shouts, and laughingly attempt to restrain her, but she nonetheless manages to snatch off MADAME PACE's *wig and fling it to the floor.*

MOTHER. You old witch! Murderer! My daughter!

STEPDAUGHTER (*rushing to restrain the* MOTHER). No, no, Mamma, no! For God's sake, no!

FATHER (*rushing up at the same time*). Calm down! Take it easy! Just sit down!

MOTHER. Get that woman out of my sight!

STEPDAUGHTER (*to the* DIRECTOR, *who has also run up*). We can't do it, it's impossible – we can't have my mother here!

FATHER (*also to the* DIRECTOR). They can't be in the same room together! That's why she wasn't with us when we first came in, don't you see? If they meet up, it gives the whole show away.

DIRECTOR. That doesn't matter. This is only a run-through at this stage. It's all grist for the mill, even if it is a bit confusing – I'll sort all the various elements out later.

Turning to the MOTHER, *he leads her to her chair and sits her back down again.*

Now come along, dear lady – take it easy. Sit down, please.

The STEPDAUGHTER *has meanwhile gone back into centre stage, and turns to address* MADAME PACE.

STEPDAUGHTER. Right, Madame Pace, go on!

MADAME PACE (*offended*). No no, *grazie tante*. I do nothing – *niente, ha capito?* – not weeth your Mamma here.

STEPDAUGHTER. Oh, don't be silly – send in this *vecchio signore* who wants to *divertirsi* with me! (*Turning rather grandly to the others.*) We've got to do this scene, that's all there is to it! Come on, let's go! (*To* MADAME PACE.) You can leave.

MADAME PACE. Oh, I go, I go for sure!

Storms out in a rage, snatching up her wig and glaring fiercely at the ACTORS, *who applaud mockingly.*

STEPDAUGHTER (*to the* FATHER). You can make your entrance now – you don't have to go round, just come straight over. Pretend you're already on. Right – I'm standing here with my head bowed – modest, you see? Now, come on – speak up! In a sort of newly-arrived voice, like somebody who's just come in from outside: 'Good afternoon, miss . . . '

DIRECTOR (*now down off the stage*). Well, really! Who's directing here, you or me? (*To the* FATHER, *who looks bemused and uncertain.*) Yes, do what she says. Go upstage, don't exit, though, then come back down.

The FATHER *does so, almost in a daze. He is very pale, but already imbued with the reality of his created life, he is smiling as he moves downstage, as if detached from the drama which is poised to overwhelm him. The* ACTORS *are suddenly intent upon the scene which is about to unfold.*

DIRECTOR (*hurriedly, in an undertone to the* PROMPTER *in his box*). Now, get ready to write!

The Scene

FATHER (*coming downstage, in character*). Good afternoon, miss.

STEPDAUGHTER (*head bowed, with barely concealed disgust*). Good afternoon.

The FATHER peers underneath the brim of her hat, which almost completely hides her face, and observing that she is extremely young, utters a cry, as if to himself, partly of satisfaction, partly of fear that he might be compromised in a tricky situation.

FATHER. Ah! Er . . . Tell me . . . This wouldn't be the first time, surely? I mean, that you've been here?

STEPDAUGHTER (*head still bowed, as before*). No, sir.

FATHER. You've been here other times? (*The STEPDAUGHTER nods.*) More than once? (*He waits a moment for her response, peers at her again under her hat, then smiles.*) Oh, well . . . You shouldn't be too . . . Perhaps you'll allow me to remove this little hat?

STEPDAUGHTER (*quickly preventing him, with a show of revulsion*). No, sir! I'll take it off myself!

The MOTHER watches the scene, along with the SON and the other two children, who are younger, and more her own, and remain constantly by her side, grouped together at the opposite side of the stage from the ACTORS. She is on tenterhooks, following the words and actions of the FATHER and STEPDAUGHTER, and displaying a range of emotions – grief, contempt, anxiety, horror. Now and again she covers her face, and utters a groan.

MOTHER. Oh, God! Oh, my God!

Hearing her groan, the FATHER freezes, as if turned to stone, for a long moment, then resumes, in character, as before.

FATHER. Here, give it to me – I'll put it down. (*Takes the hat from her hand.*) Hm . . . a pretty little head like yours should have a decent hat, something more worthy of it. If you'd like to help me choose one of Madame Pace's . . . No?

INGENUE (*interrupting*). Hey, hang on a minute! Those are *our* hats!

DIRECTOR (*angrily*). Be quiet, for God's sake! Never mind the jokes! This is the key scene*!* (*To the* STEPDAUGHTER.) Right, carry on, please.

STEPDAUGHTER (*continuing*). No, sir – no, thank you.

FATHER. Oh, come now, don't refuse me. Accept one, please do. I'll be terribly disappointed. Look, these are lovely, aren't they. And Madame Pace'll be delighted. That's why she puts them out on display.

STEPDAUGHTER. No, sir. I couldn't possibly wear one.

FATHER. Why not? Is it because of what they might think at home, if they see you with a new hat? Good heavens – don't you know what to say? You can talk your way out of that, surely?

STEPDAUGHTER (*frantic, at her wits' end*). No, sir, no, it's not that! I *can't* wear it, because . . . well, look at me! Look, you must've noticed! (*Shows him her black dress.*)

FATHER. In mourning, of course! I beg your pardon, I'm so sorry – yes, I can see now. I'm absolutely mortified, believe me.

STEPDAUGHTER (*mustering up all her strength to overcome her contempt and revulsion*). No, stop, stop! I should actually be thanking you, you shouldn't be feeling mortified or upset. Don't pay any attention to what I've just said. That goes for me too — you see? (*Forces a smile, and adds.*) I shouldn't even be aware I'm dressed like this.

DIRECTOR (*interrupts, climbing back up onto the stage and addressing the* PROMPTER *in his box*). Hold on, wait! Don't write that down — cross out that last line. (*To the* FATHER *and* STEPDAUGHTER.) You're doing fine, that's excellent! (*Then to the* FATHER *alone.*) Now we'll put in that little bit as we discussed. (*To the* ACTORS.) That's quite charming, that scene with the hat, don't you think?

STEPDAUGHTER. But the best is yet to come — why don't we just carry on?

DIRECTOR. Be patient a moment. (*To the* ACTORS *again.*) This'll need a light touch, of course.

LEADING MAN. Oh, for sure — a little more upbeat.

LEADING LADY. Well, obviously — that'll be no problem. (*To the* LEADING MAN.) Why don't we run it through now?

LEADING MAN. Fine by me. Right, I'll go off and get ready to enter.

Goes out and prepares to re-enter by the upstage door.

DIRECTOR (*to the* LEADING LADY.) Now then, that's the scene with you and Madame Pace finished — I'll get it written up later. So you stay here . . . wait, where are you going?

LEADING LADY. Hang on, I've got to put my hat back on . . . (*Takes her hat from the rack and does so.*)

DIRECTOR. Yes, of course – that's excellent. Right – you stand over here now with your head bowed.

STEPDAUGHTER (*amused*). But she's not wearing black, is she.

LEADING LADY. Oh, I'll be wearing black, don't worry – and I'll look better in it than you!

DIRECTOR (*to the* STEPDAUGHTER). Be quiet, please! Just watch. Look and learn, right? (*Clapping his hands.*) Now – let's go! Enter!

He climbs back down from the stage in order to get an impression of the scene. The upstage door opens and the LEADING MAN *makes his entrance in a devil-may-care, self-assured manner, like an aging roué. From the very first lines, it will be clear that the* ACTORS *are playing the scene quite differently – without, however, any suggestion of parody; rather, this is the 'new improved version'. Naturally, the* STEPDAUGHTER *and* FATHER *are unable to recognise themselves in the* LEADING LADY *and* LEADING MAN, *and as they hear their own words spoken, they variously express their reactions, of surprise, astonishment, pain, etc., now and again smiling, or gesturing, or openly protesting. The voice of the* PROMPTER *can be clearly heard from his box.*

LEADING MAN. 'Good afternoon, miss . . . '

FATHER (*suddenly, unable to contain himself*) No, no!

Seeing the LEADING MAN *enter in this manner, the* STEPDAUGHTER *bursts out laughing.*

DIRECTOR (*enraged*). Silence, dammit! And you can stop that laughing right now, d'you hear? We can't go on like this!

STEPDAUGHTER (*coming downstage*). You'll forgive me, sir, but I can't help it. That young lady (*Indicating the* LEADING LADY.) is standing quite calmly, where she's been put, but I can assure you – if it were me, and somebody said, 'Good afternoon', to me like that, in that tone of voice, well, I'd have burst out laughing, exactly as I just did!

FATHER (*also coming downstage a little way*). That's right! It's his manner, the tone of voice . . .

DIRECTOR. What d'you mean, 'manner'? What tone of voice? Look, stand out of the way, and let me see the rehearsal!

LEADING MAN (*coming forward*). Well, if I'm supposed to be playing an old man, who comes into a house of ill-repute . . .

DIRECTOR. Yes, yes, of course – never mind them, for God's sake! Now, let's pick it up from there – it's going very nicely. (*Waiting for the* LEADING MAN *to continue.*) Well? Go on . . .

LEADING MAN. 'Good afternoon, miss . . . '

LEADING LADY. 'Good afternoon . . . '

The LEADING MAN *imitates the gesture of the* FATHER, *of peeking underneath her hat, but this time expresses quite distinctly first his satisfaction, then his fear.*

LEADING MAN. 'Ah! Er . . . Tell me . . . This wouldn't be the first time, I'm sure . . . '

FATHER (*correcting him, unable to resist*). No no – not 'I'm sure'. He says 'surely?'.

DIRECTOR. Yes, say 'surely?' – it's a question.

LEADING MAN (*looking meaningfully at the* PROMPTER).
Well, I heard it as 'I'm sure'.

DIRECTOR. Oh, what's the difference? 'Surely' or 'I'm
sure' – just get on with it. And a little less stagy, if you
would. Look, I'll show you. Watch . . . (*Climbs up on stage,
then replays the part, starting from the entrance.*) 'Good
afternoon, miss . . . '

LEADING LADY. 'Good afternoon . . . '

DIRECTOR. 'Ah! Er . . . Tell me . . . ' (*Turning to the*
LEADING MAN *to show him how he should look at the*
LEADING LADY *under her hat.*) Surprise, you see?
Fear, but also satisfaction . . . (*Then continues the scene, to
the* LEADING LADY.) 'This wouldn't be the first time,
surely? I mean, that you've been here . . . ?' (*To the*
LEADING MAN *again, questioningly.*) Clear? (*To the*
LEADING LADY.) Then you say, 'No, sir.' (*To the*
LEADING MAN, *once more.*) I'm not sure how to explain
it – basically more relaxed. (*Climbs back down off the stage.*)

LEADING LADY. 'No, sir . . . '

LEADING MAN. 'You've been here other times? More
than once?'

DIRECTOR. No no, wait! You've got to let her nod first.
(*Indicating the* LEADING LADY.) Right – 'You've been
here other times?'

The LEADING LADY *raises her head a little, eyes half-closed
in a show of pain and revulsion, and on a cue of 'Now' from the*
DIRECTOR, *nods twice.*

STEPDAUGHTER (*unable to help herself*). Oh, my God! (*Hurriedly claps her hand over her mouth to stifle a laugh.*)

DIRECTOR (*turning round*). What's the matter?

STEPDAUGHTER (*hastily*). Nothing, nothing!

DIRECTOR (*to the* LEADING MAN). That's your cue – go on, go on!

LEADING MAN. 'More than once? Oh, well . . . You shouldn't be too . . . Perhaps you'll allow me to remove this little hat?'

Delivering these lines, the LEADING MAN's *mannered speech and gestures send the* STEPDAUGHTER *into a fit of helpless laughter, which she is unable to contain, despite having her hand still clamped over her mouth.*

LEADING LADY (*storms back to her seat, indignant*). Look, I'm not going to stand here and let her make a fool of me!

LEADING MAN. Nor me! That's it, I'm finished!

DIRECTOR (*to the* STEPDAUGHTER, *shouting*). That's enough, dammit!

STEPDAUGHTER. Right, right – I'm sorry . . .

DIRECTOR. That's extremely rude of you – that's ignorant, that's what it is! How you have the nerve to . . .

FATHER (*trying to intervene*). You're right, sir, you're absolutely right – but you've got to forgive her . . .

DIRECTOR (*climbing back up onto the stage*). Forgive her? I'm damned if I will – it's a disgrace!

FATHER. Yes, sir, yes – but honestly, all this is having a really strange effect on us . . .

DIRECTOR. Strange? What d'you mean, strange? In what way?

FATHER. Sir, I've nothing but admiration for your actors – truly – but that gentleman (*Indicates the* LEADING MAN), and this lady here (*Indicates the* LEADING LADY) – well, sir, I do assure you – they're not us . . .

DIRECTOR. Well, of course they're not! How the hell could they be 'you', if they're actors?

FATHER. Yes, that's just my point – they're actors! And they're playing us really rather well, both of them. But obviously, from our point of view, they're something quite different – they would like to be the same, but they just aren't.

DIRECTOR. So why aren't they? What's the matter now?

FATHER. It's the fact that . . . well, it's *them* now, and no longer us.

DIRECTOR. Yes, obviously – that's how it works. I've told you that already!

FATHER. Yes, I know, I know.

DIRECTOR. Right, then – that's enough. (*Turning to the* ACTORS *again.*) We'll rehearse this later in private, same as usual. It's sheer hell rehearsing with the author present – they're never happy! (*Turning back to the* FATHER *and* STEPDAUGHTER.) Right, we'll give it another try with you two – and without the laughter this time, if you please.

STEPDAUGHTER. I won't laugh again, honestly! This is my best bit coming up – just wait!

DIRECTOR. So – when you say, 'Don't pay any attention to
what I've just said. That goes for me too, you see . . . '
(*To the* FATHER.) you come in quickly with, 'Ah, yes –
I understand . . . ' and then you immediately ask her . . .

STEPDAUGHTER (*interrupting*). Ask me what?

DIRECTOR. Why you're in mourning.

STEPDAUGHTER. Oh, no, sir, no! In point of fact, when
I told him he needn't be concerned with what I was
wearing, d'you know what he said? 'That's splendid,' he
said, 'Let's take this little black dress off right now!'

DIRECTOR. Oh, that's just beautiful – excellent! What,
d'you want the audience jumping out of their seats?

STEPDAUGHTER. But it's the truth!

DIRECTOR. The truth? Oh, please! This is the theatre –
truth up to a point, yes!

STEPDAUGHTER. Well, I'm sorry, but what d'you want
me to do, then?

DIRECTOR. You'll see, you'll see. Just let me get on with it.

STEPDAUGHTER. No, sir, I won't. Are you really going
to take this feeling of nausea I have, from all the vile and
humiliating experiences that have made me the person
I am, and whip it up into some sickly-sweet little romance,
in which he asks me why I'm in mourning, and I tell
him, with tears in my eyes, that poor daddy died two
months ago? No no, my dear sir! He's got to say what
he actually said: 'That's splendid – let's take this little
black dress off right now!' And then I, grief-stricken, in
mourning for barely two months, went over there, d'you

see? Behind that screen, and with my fingers trembling with shame, with revulsion – took off my dress and corset. . . .

DIRECTOR (*running his fingers through his hair*). For God's sake! What are you saying?

STEPDAUGHTER (*frantic, shouting*). The truth, sir! The truth!

DIRECTOR. Well, yes, of course, I'm not denying it's the truth – and I do understand the horror you feel, young lady, believe me. But *you've* got to understand that we can't do all this on stage – it's not possible!

STEPDAUGHTER. Not possible? Right, then – thank you very much, but I've had enough!

DIRECTOR. No no, wait – look . . .

STEPDAUGHTER. I've had enough, I'm leaving! You've worked it all out back there, haven't you, the pair of you – just what's possible on stage. Well, that's nice – I know exactly what's happening here – he wants to run on ahead to his big scene, his big moment of 'spiritual anguish'! But I want to act out *my* part, *my* drama!

DIRECTOR (*irritated, with a haughty shrug*). Oh, I see – *your* drama! Well, I'm sorry, but it isn't just yours. There are other parts too. His, for a start (*Indicating the* FATHER), and your mother's! You can't have one character hogging the limelight, and upstaging everybody else. You've got to maintain some sort of balanced ensemble, to show what needs to be shown. And I'm perfectly well aware that we all have our own inner life, that we'd love to open up to the world. But that's what's so difficult – we have to bring out only what's essential, in relation to the other characters, and somehow use that to hint at the life within. I mean, it would be just too convenient if every character was allowed a soliloquy – or better still, a lecture – to dish up to the audience whatever's cooking inside them! (*Then gently, more conciliatory.*) You need to restrain yourself, my dear. It's in your own best interest, believe me. Otherwise, I must warn you, it's likely to make a bad impression – all this self-lacerating fury, all this fired-up disgust – I mean, you've already admitted to having been with other men before him at Madame Pace's – and more than once!

STEPDAUGHTER (*pausing to reflect, then in a low voice, her head bowed*). That's true. But bear in mind, all those other men were equally *him,* as far as I was concerned.

DIRECTOR. The other men? What do you mean?

STEPDAUGHTER. Sir, when someone goes to the bad, isn't it the person that first set them on that sinful path, who is ultimately responsible for their fall from grace? And for me, that was him – even before I was born. Just look at him, and see if that isn't true!

DIRECTOR. Right, fair enough. But don't you think that's a burden on his conscience? At least give him the chance to show it.

STEPDAUGHTER. So tell me, please – how exactly is he going to show all these fine feelings of remorse, all these so-called moral 'torments' of his, if you're planning to spare him the horror of finding himself one fine day in the arms of a woman – a fallen woman at that – having just asked her to take off her dress – her black mourning

dress – only to discover that she's that same little girl, sir,
the one he used to watch coming out of school!

She speaks these last words in a voice trembling with emotion.
Hearing her say this, the MOTHER *is suddenly overwhelmed by*
grief, expressed at first in a few choking sobs, then uncontrollable
weeping. Everyone is profoundly moved. A long pause. The
STEPDAUGHTER *waits until the* MOTHER *shows signs of*
calming down, then continues, in a sombre, resolute manner.

STEPDAUGHTER. We're still just amongst ourselves here
at the moment, unknown to the public. Tomorrow you'll
put on a performance, and I dare say you'll make use of
us however you please. But wouldn't you like to see the
real drama? See it burst into life, the way it really was?

DIRECTOR. Yes, of course – there's nothing I'd like better.
That way I'll get as much out of it as possible.

STEPDAUGHTER. Right, then – you'll have to send the
Mother out.

MOTHER (*her tears giving way to a shriek*). No, no! Don't let
her do it, sir! Don't let her!

DIRECTOR. But it's just so we can see it, dear lady.

MOTHER. No, I can't bear it! I can't!

DIRECTOR. But if it's all happened already . . . ? I'm
sorry, I don't understand.

MOTHER. No, it's happening now, it's happening all the
time! My suffering's not an act, sir, I'm living through it
here and now, always – every moment of my agony,
constantly renewing itself, now and forever. And those
two children – you've never heard them speak, have

you? That's because they can't! Yes, they're still here, clinging onto me, keeping my pain alive, but for themselves, they no longer exist! And this one, sir – (*Indicating the* STEPDAUGHTER.) this one's run away, she's abandoned me completely, and now she's lost – yes, lost . . . And if I'm seeing her here now, it's for one reason, and one reason only – to renew my agony, to keep the pain I've suffered on her behalf alive for ever and ever.

FATHER (*gravely*). It's the eternal moment, sir – I spoke about it earlier. She (*Indicating the* STEPDAUGHTER.) is here to trap me, to fix me in that moment, dangling there for all eternity, pilloried for one shameful fleeting instant in my life! She can't let it go, and in truth, sir, you can't save me from it.

DIRECTOR. Oh yes, I'm not saying we won't show that bit. Indeed no, it'll form the nucleus of the entire first act, up to the point when she (*Indicating the* MOTHER.) walks in on you.

FATHER. Yes, that's right, sir. Because this is the moment when I am finally condemned – all our suffering has to culminate in that scream of hers! (*Again indicating the* MOTHER.)

STEPDAUGHTER. Oh God, it still rings in my ears! It's driven me mad, that scream. You can show me on stage any way you like, sir, I don't care. Fully dressed, if you want, as long as I have at least my arms bare, just the arms. Because you see – look – standing here, (*Goes up to the* FATHER *and lays her head against his chest.*) with my head in this position, and my arms round his neck like

so, I could see a vein throbbing in my arm, just here.
And it was as if that throbbing vein, and not anything
else, filled me with revulsion, and I shut my eyes tight,
like this, and buried my head in his chest. (*Turning towards
the* MOTHER.) Scream, Mamma, scream!

She buries her head in the FATHER's *chest, and with her
shoulders hunched, as if trying to block out the scream, calls out, in
an agonized, muffled voice.*

Scream, Mamma, the way you did then!

MOTHER (*rushing forward to separate them*). No! It's my
daughter, my daughter! (*Pulling her away from him.*) You beast!
She's my daughter! Can't you see she's my daughter?

At this outburst, the DIRECTOR *backs off downstage, as far as
the footlights, while the* ACTORS *register alarm.*

DIRECTOR. Excellent! That's excellent! And now the
curtain!

FATHER (*running up to him, agitated*). Yes, that's it! That's just
how it was, sir!

DIRECTOR (*enthusiastically, impressed*). Yes, of course! That's
got to be it – and then the curtain! The curtain!

At the DIRECTOR's *repeated shouts of 'Curtain!', the*
TECHNICIAN *lowers the curtain, leaving the* DIRECTOR
and the FATHER *in front of it, at the footlights.*

DIRECTOR (*looking up to the heavens, his hands in the air*). Idiots!
When I said 'Curtain!' I meant that was the curtain *line*,
and they've gone and dropped the damn thing! (*Lifting up
one end of the curtain to allow them to get back on stage.*)
Anyway, that's first class! A guaranteed effect – that's our

curtain, it's got to be. Yes, yes, that first act's a surefire winner! (*Goes back behind the curtain with the* FATHER.)

When the curtain is raised again, we see that the STAGEHANDS *have dismantled the first set, and replaced it with a small garden pond with a fountain. The* ACTORS *are seated in a row at one side of the stage, and the* CHARACTERS *at the other. The* DIRECTOR *is standing centre stage, his clenched fist pressed against his mouth as if deep in thought.*

DIRECTOR (*stirring, after a brief pause*). Right . . . now . . . let's get on to Act Two. Just leave it to me, the way we agreed, and everything'll be fine.

STEPDAUGHTER. This is where we come to live with, him (*Indicating the* FATHER.) despite his objections! (*Indicating the* SON.)

DIRECTOR (*testily*). Yes, yes, I know. Just leave it to me, will you?

STEPDAUGHTER. Yes, but you've got to make his resentment clear.

MOTHER (*in her corner, shaking her head*). For all the good that's come out of it . . .

STEPDAUGHTER (*rounding on her*). That doesn't matter. The more damage done to us, the guiltier he feels!

DIRECTOR (*impatiently*). All right, all right, I get the point! I'll bear it mind, especially at the beginning. So don't worry.

MOTHER (*pleading*). And please, sir, I beg you – to ease my conscience, make it clear that I tried every way I could, to . . .

STEPDAUGHTER (*scornfully interrupting her*). . . . To pacify me, to try and persuade me that all that beastliness wasn't worth it! (*To the* DIRECTOR.) Do what she says, make her happy, because it's all true! I'm really enjoying this, as you can see. The more effort she makes to ingratiate herself, to worm her way into his heart, the more remote he becomes – a virtual absentee! Choice, isn't it?

DIRECTOR. Look, d'you think we might make a start on this second act?

STEPDAUGHTER. I won't say another word. Just let me warn you that you won't be able to stage it all in the garden, if that's what you're intending – it won't be possible.

DIRECTOR. What d'you mean, not possible?

STEPDAUGHTER. Because he (*Indicating the* SON *again.*) spends all his time shut up in his room, isolated! Besides which, all the scenes involving this poor, confused little boy take place in the house, as I've already told you.

DIRECTOR. Well, yes, of course, but we can't put up signs or change the scenery three or four times in one act.

STEPDAUGHTER. Why not? That's what they used to do.

DIRECTOR. Yes, when the audience was about as sophisticated as that little girl there!

LEADING LADY. And it was easier to create an illusion.

FATHER (*suddenly, leaping to his feet*). Illusion? For God's sake, don't say illusion. Don't even mention that word to us – it's too painful!

DIRECTOR (*astonished*). I beg your pardon?

FATHER. It is, it's such a cruel word! Surely you understand?

DIRECTOR. So what are we supposed to say, then? That's what we do here – create an illusion, for the audience . . .

LEADING MAN. Through our performance . . .

DIRECTOR. An illusion of reality!

FATHER. Yes, I understand that, sir. But perhaps you don't understand us. I'm sorry, but as far as you and your actors are concerned, all this is just a game – and that's as it should be.

LEADING LADY (*interrupting indignantly*). What d'you mean, game? We're not children, you know! We're serious actors!

FATHER. I'm not saying you aren't. What I actually mean is that your art is a kind of game, in which you try very hard to present – as the gentleman says – a perfect illusion of reality.

DIRECTOR. Yes, that's it, precisely.

FATHER. But if you stop to consider, sir – the six of us standing here (*Indicates himself and the other five* CHARACTERS.) . . . well, we have no other reality *outside* that illusion!

DIRECTOR (*astonished, looks across at his* ACTORS, *equally bewildered*). What on earth d'you mean?

FATHER (*observing them for a moment, with a wan smile*). Just that, sirs. What other reality do we have? What for you is an illusion to be created, is for us our unique reality.

(*A brief pause, then moves a few paces towards the* DIRECTOR.) But that doesn't only apply to us, if you think about it. (*Looks into his eyes.*) I mean, can you tell me who *you* are? (*Pointing at the* DIRECTOR.)

DIRECTOR (*taken aback, with a faint smile*). What? Who *I* am? I'm me!

FATHER. And what if I were to say that's not true, because you're *me?*

DIRECTOR. I'd say you were crazy! (*The* ACTORS *laugh.*)

FATHER. They're quite right to laugh, because this is a game we're playing here. (*To the* DIRECTOR.) And of course you'll argue that it's simply part of the game, that that gentleman over there, who is in fact himself, should be *me,* while I, on the contrary, am myself – but that's where I've caught you out, don't you see? (*The* ACTORS *start laughing again.*)

DIRECTOR (*irritated*). But we've already said all this. D'you want us to go over it again?

FATHER. No no, that's not really what I meant. What I'd like you to do is to drop this game of yours . . . (*Looking at the* LEADING LADY, *as if to forestall her.*) all right, this art, this art! . . . which you're so used to creating here with your actors, and give serious consideration to the question: who are you?

DIRECTOR (*astonished, and also irritated, turning to the* ACTORS). Well, that takes some nerve! Sets himself up as a character, then has the gall to ask me who I am!

FATHER (*dignified, but with no show of arrogance*). My dear sir, a character can always ask a man who he is. Because a character genuinely has a life of his own, distinguished by its own individual characteristics, which means that he is always 'somebody'. A man, on the other hand – I'm not saying you in particular, but man in general – can be 'nobody'.

DIRECTOR. Yes, all right. But you're asking me, sir, the director! The man in charge! Do you understand?

FATHER (*almost in a whisper, with honeyed deference*). All I wanted to know, sir, was whether you truly see yourself now the same way as you did at some point in the past, for example – what you were like back then, with all the illusions you had at that time – all those things in and around you as they appeared when they were still so real to you. Well, sir, if you think back to those illusions, which you no longer possess – all those things which no longer 'appear' to be quite what they 'were' . . . well, don't you feel the ground – I don't mean this stage – but the earth itself, the solid ground beneath your feet, about to give way? I mean, when you come to think of it – in exactly the same fashion, 'this' – what you feel at this moment, the entire reality of today, as it is now – is fated to seem an illusion tomorrow.

DIRECTOR (*not fully comprehending, but dazzled by the specious argument*). Well? What does that prove?

FATHER. Oh, nothing, nothing, sir. It's just to show you that if we (*Again indicates himself and the other* CHARACTERS.) have no other reality beyond illusion, then you too would do well not to trust in your own reality – the living and breathing reality you enjoy today – because just like yesterday's reality, that too is destined to be exposed as an illusion tomorrow.

DIRECTOR (*setting out to make fun of him*). Oh, that's very good! So what you're saying is that you, and this play you've come here to perform, are actually more real than I am?

FATHER (*deadly serious*). Beyond a shadow of doubt, sir!

DIRECTOR. What?

FATHER. I thought you understood that right from the start.

DIRECTOR. More real than me?

FATHER. Well, if your reality can change, from one day to the next . . .

DIRECTOR. Good God, of course it can change! It changes all the time – same as everybody else's!

FATHER (*shouts*). No, sir – not ours! You see? That's the difference. Ours doesn't change, it can't change – it can never be any different, because it's fixed like this forever – and that's the horror of it, sir! Immutable reality – why, it should make you shudder even to come near us!

The DIRECTOR, *as if suddenly struck by an idea out of the blue, goes over to confront the* FATHER.

DIRECTOR. Now, what I'd like to know, is when anybody's ever seen a character step out of the part he's supposed to be playing, and start pontificating about it the way you're doing – offering interpretations and what not? Can you tell me that, sir? Because that's quite unheard of, in my experience!

FATHER. Well, you haven't encountered it before, sir, because authors generally try to keep their creative processes hidden. When the characters are alive, truly alive, standing in front of their creator, all he has to do is follow the words and actions they suggest to him. He's got to want them to be the way *they* want. And if he doesn't, well, that's just too bad. Once a character's born, he immediately assumes so much independence, even from his own creator, that he can be imagined in all kinds of different situations, which would never have crossed the author's mind, and sometimes he even takes on a significance the author would never have dreamed of giving him!

DIRECTOR. Of course, I know that.

FATHER. So what's so surprising about us? Just think what a disaster it is for a character such as I've described – to be born into the world from the imagination of an author, who then tries to deny him life – and then tell me if a character left like this, alive and yet lifeless, hasn't every right to do exactly what we're doing now, standing here in front of you, having done the same thing, over and over again, believe me, trying to persuade him, urging him on – if not me, then her (*Indicating the* STEPDAUGHTER), or that poor mother there . . .

STEPDAUGHTER (*coming forward as if in a trance*). It's true, sir. I did it too. I tried so many times to tempt him, when he was feeling depressed in his study at twilight, slumped in an armchair, unable to decide whether or not to turn on the lights, and allowing the shadows to invade the room – shadows that were swarming with ourselves, coming to tempt him.

It is as if she still sees herself there in that study, and is annoyed by the presence of all these ACTORS.

If only you people would go away! If only you'd leave us
alone! The mother there, with that son of hers − myself
with that little girl − that little boy, always on his own −
then myself and him − (*Vaguely indicating the* FATHER.)
and then myself alone . . . all alone, in the shadows.
(*Gives a sudden start, as if trying to catch hold of that vision she
has of herself, radiant and alive in the shadows.*) Oh, my life!
What scenes, what scenes we suggested to him! And I was
the one who tempted him most of all!

FATHER. Yes, indeed. But maybe it was your fault −
precisely because you kept on and on at him, you didn't
know when to stop!

STEPDAUGHTER. That's nonsense! That was the way he
wanted me. (*Goes up close to the* DIRECTOR *to speak to him
in confidence.*) Actually, sir, I think it was more out of
disillusionment with the theatre, or contempt for it − the
sort of stuff audiences today seem to want . . .

DIRECTOR. Anyway, let's get on with it, for God's sake.
Let's get down to business!

STEPDAUGHTER. Sir, if you don't mind me saying −
I think we've got too many things on the go, with our
moving into his house. (*Indicating the* FATHER.) I mean,
you said you couldn't put up signs, or change the scenery
every five minutes.

DIRECTOR. No, of course not! Exactly. We need to run
them together, group them into one continuous action −
and not the way you're expecting. You'd like to see your
little brother first, coming home from school and
wandering through the house like a spectre, lurking

behind the doors and brooding on some sort of plan, whereby he . . . how did you put it?

STEPDAUGHTER. Shrivels up, sir – shrivels up completely!

DIRECTOR. Hm – that's a new one on me. Well, anyway – 'only his eyes keep on growing' – is that it?

STEPDAUGHTER. Yes, sir. Look at him. (*Indicating the* YOUNG BOY *beside his* MOTHER.)

DIRECTOR. Yes, very nice. Then at the same time you want us to see that little girl, playing innocently in the garden – one inside the house, the other in the garden, right?

STEPDAUGHTER. Yes, sir – in the sunshine, so happy! That's my sole reward – her happiness, her joy in that garden, away from all the misery, the squalor of that dreadful room we had to sleep in, all four of us. With me alongside her – just imagine it – the horror of my vile, contaminated body next to hers, as she held me tight, so tight, in those loving, innocent little arms. In the garden, as soon as she saw me, she would run up and take me by the hand. She wouldn't even glance at the big flowers – instead she'd go looking for all the 'teeny-weeny' ones, desperate to show them to me, so happy, so excited!

At this point, tormented by the pain of recollection, she breaks into prolonged, desperate weeping, letting her head drop onto her arms, outspread on the little table. Everyone is deeply moved. The DIRECTOR *goes over to her, in an almost fatherly manner, and tries to comfort her.*

DIRECTOR. We'll do the garden scene, don't worry, we'll do it. And you'll be delighted with it. We'll set the whole

thing in the garden! (*Calls to a* STAGEHAND *by name.*)
Hoi! Drop a couple of tree-pieces down here, will you?
Two little cypresses in front of the pond.

Two small cypresses are lowered from the flies onto the stage. The
TECHNICIAN *runs up and nails down the two bases.*

DIRECTOR (*to the* STEPDAUGHTER). This'll do for the
moment – give us an idea. (*Calls to the* STAGEHAND
again by name.) Hoi! Let's have a bit of sky too, eh?

STAGEHAND (*from above*). What's that?

DIRECTOR. A bit of sky! A sky-flat – drop it in here
behind the pond!

A white back-cloth is lowered from the flies onto the stage.

DIRECTOR. No, not white! I said sky! Oh, never mind,
just leave it. I'll fix it. (*Calling.*) Hoi, electrician! Let's have
all these lights out, and give me a bit of atmosphere . . .
a bit of moonlight . . . blue, the blues on the batten, and
a blue spot on the cloth . . . That'll do, that's fine!

*At his command, a mysterious moonlit scene is created, which makes
the* ACTORS *speak and move as if they were in a garden at
night, beneath the moon.*

DIRECTOR (*to the* STEPDAUGHTER). There you are,
you see? So instead of lurking behind doors inside the
house, the young lad can now wander about the garden
and hide behind the trees. But you'll have to understand
it's not going to be easy finding a little girl to make a
decent job of that scene with you, when she shows you
the flowers. (*Turning to the* YOUNG BOY.) Come down
here a minute – let's see if we can work this out. (*And*

when the YOUNG BOY *doesn't move.*) Come on, come on! (*He then pulls him forward, trying to make him hold up his head, which keeps dropping onto his chest.*) Oh, this is wonderful! What the hell's the matter with the boy? I mean, for God's sake, he's got to say *something!* (*He goes up to him, puts his arm round him and leads him behind the trees.*) Right, come on. Let's see what we can do. You hide round here for a bit . . . That's it . . . Now – poke your head out as if you were spying on somebody . . . (*He stands back to watch the effect, and the* YOUNG BOY *does as he is bidden, rather to the surprise of the* ACTORS, *who are impressed.*) Excellent! Splendid! (*Turning to the* STEPDAUGHTER.) Now – what if the little girl were to catch him peeping out and run over to him? We might get a word or two out of him that way.

STEPDAUGHTER (*leaping to her feet*). Not a hope. He won't open his mouth while *he*'s here. (*Indicating the* SON.) You'll have to get rid of *him* first.

SON (*making his way promptly towards one of the two little staircases*). Suits me – no sooner said than done! With pleasure!

DIRECTOR (*hurrying to stop him*). No! Where are you going? Hold on!

Upset and alarmed by the thought that he might really be leaving, the MOTHER *instinctively lifts up her arms to restrain him, without however moving from the spot.*

SON (*to the* DIRECTOR, *who has stopped him at the footlights*). I've got absolutely nothing to do with all this. Let me go, please! Just let me leave!

DIRECTOR. What d'you mean, nothing to do with it?

STEPDAUGHTER (*calmly, with heavy irony*). Oh, don't hold him back. He won't go anyway.

FATHER. He's got to play that terrible scene in the garden with his mother.

SON (*vehemently, determined*). I'm not playing anything! I said that right at the beginning! (*To the* DIRECTOR.) Let me go!

STEPDAUGHTER (*rushing up to the* DIRECTOR). Allow me, sir! (*She makes him lower his arms, restraining the* SON.) Now, let him go. (*To the* SON, *as soon as the* DIRECTOR *has released him.*) Well? Go on, go!

The SON *remains poised to descend the staircase, but it is as if he is being held back by some mysterious power, and he is unable to do so. Then, while the* ACTORS *look on in anxious disbelief, he edges slowly along the footlights, towards the other little staircase leading down from the stage. When he reaches it, however, he again remains rooted to the spot, unable to descend. The* STEPDAUGHTER, *watching all this intently, in an attitude of defiance, bursts out laughing.*

He can't do it, you see? He can't! He's got to stay here, he's forced to – bound by a chain that can't be broken. If I'm the one that runs away, when the inevitable happens – precisely because of the hatred I feel for him, precisely because of never wanting to see him again – well, if I'm still here, if I can stand the sight of him, and bear his presence, how can you imagine he has any right to leave? He's the one who really *has* to stay, with that wonderful father of his, and that mother, who has no other son *but* him! (*Turning to the* MOTHER.) Oh, come on, Mamma, get up – come on! (*Turning to the* DIRECTOR *to point at her.*) Look, you see? She was getting up – she was getting up to hold him back. (*To the* MOTHER, *as if drawing her forward by some magical power.*) Come . . . Come . . . (*Then to the* DIRECTOR.) Think how she hates having to show her feelings in front of your actors. But she's so desperate to be near him, that . . . there you are, you see? She's even willing to play out her scene!

Indeed, the MOTHER *is already with her* SON, *and as the* STEPDAUGHTER *utters these last words, the* MOTHER *gestures to signify her consent.*

SON (*hurriedly*). No no, not me! I won't do it! If I can't leave, then I'll stay here, but I'm not acting out anything, I've told you!

FATHER (*to the* DIRECTOR, *agitated*). You can make him do it, sir!

SON. Nobody can make me do anything!

FATHER. I'll damn well make you!

STEPDAUGHTER. Wait! Wait! The little girl has to be at the pond first!

She runs over to get the LITTLE GIRL, *kneels down before her and holds her face between her hands.*

Oh, my poor little darling – you look so lost with those beautiful big eyes of yours. You haven't a clue where you are, have you. We're on a stage, my darling! And what's a stage? Well, don't you see? It's a place where you play at being serious. A place where you act out a play. And

that's what we're going to do now – play, only seriously.
And you too . . .

*She puts her arms round her and hugs her tight, gently rocking her
to and fro a moment.*

Oh, my dearest darling child, what a frightful play this
is for you! What a horrible part they've dreamed up for
you! The garden, the pond . . . This is all make-believe,
you know. And that's just the trouble, my darling –
everything's fake here. Still, maybe you'd rather have a
fake pond than a real one? I mean, you could play in it,
couldn't you. But it's only a game for the others – for
you, unfortunately, it's all too real, because you're real,
my darling, and you really *are* playing in a real pond –
a beautiful big green pond, with lots of shady bamboo
reflecting in the water, and oh, lots and lots of little ducks
paddling around, making ripples in the reflections. And
you'd love to catch one, one of those little ducks . . .
(*With a sudden, terrifying shriek.*) No, Rosetta, no! Mamma
can't look after you, she's too wrapped up in her swine of
a son! I'm going crazy, my head's full of demons! And
that creature there . . .

She lets go of the LITTLE GIRL *and turns to the* YOUNG
BOY *with her customary scowl.*

What are you hanging around for, like some sort of
wretched beggar? It'll be your fault as well, if this poor
little girl drowns. There's no need for that face – by God,
I've paid plenty to get you all into this house!

She grabs him by the arm, trying to force his hand out of his pocket.

What's that you've got? What's that you're hiding? Come
on, let's see that hand!

She pulls his hand out of his pocket, and to everyone's horror, discovers that he is clutching a small revolver. She gives him a look almost of triumph, before continuing, gravely.

Aha! Now where – and how – did you get hold of that?

The YOUNG BOY, *terrified, his eyes staring and vacant as ever, does not answer.*

You idiot! If it'd been me, I'd have killed one of those two – or both of them, father and son – not myself!

She thrusts him back behind the little cypress tree from where he had been spying. She then takes the LITTLE GIRL *and places her in the pond, laying her flat so that she is hidden from view. Finally the* STEPDAUGHTER *sinks to her knees, burying her face in her arms, resting on the edge of the pond.*

DIRECTOR. Excellent! (*Turning to the* SON.) Now, meanwhile . . .

SON (*contemptuously*). Meanwhile nothing! This isn't true, sir. There never *was* any scene between me and her. (*Indicating the* MOTHER.) She'll tell you the same thing herself.

Meanwhile the SECOND ACTRESS *and the* JUVENILE LEAD *have detached themselves from the main group of* ACTORS. *The former has begun to observe the* MOTHER, *who is opposite her, very intently, while the latter does likewise with the* SON, *in preparation for playing their parts later on.*

MOTHER. Yes, that's true, sir! I'd just gone into his room.

SON. My room, did you hear that? Not into the garden!

DIRECTOR. That doesn't matter. I've already told you, we need to re-organise the action.

SON (*noticing the* JUVENILE LEAD *observing him*). What do you want?

JUVENILE LEAD. Nothing. I'm just watching.

SON (*turning round, to the* SECOND ACTRESS). Aha – and you're here too? Getting ready to play *her*. (*Indicating the* MOTHER.)

DIRECTOR. Exactly! That's it exactly. And if you ask me, you should be grateful for all the attention they're giving you.

SON. Oh, really? Well, thank you so much. You still haven't got the message, have you – you can't put on this play. There's absolutely nothing of us inside you, and these actors of yours only see us from the outside. I mean, how can we possibly live in front of a mirror, which doesn't just freeze our expression – that's bad enough – but distorts it, beyond all recognition, and actually flings it back at us as a horrible grimace?

FATHER. That's true! That's absolutely true! He's quite right.

DIRECTOR (*to the* JUVENILE LEAD *and the* SECOND ACTRESS). Fine. You two go back.

SON. Anyway, it's pointless. I'm not getting involved.

DIRECTOR. Look, be quiet, will you – I want to hear your mother. (*To the* MOTHER.) Right, then – you'd gone into his room . . .

MOTHER. Yes, sir – into his room, because I couldn't stand it any longer. I wanted to pour out my heart to him, all the sorrow that was weighing down on me. But the minute he saw me . . .

SON. Nothing happened! There was no scene whatsoever. I walked out – I left the room because I didn't want a scene. So I'm not involved, do you understand?

MOTHER. That's true! That's how it was.

DIRECTOR. Well, we'll just have to invent a scene between the two of you. It's crucial!

MOTHER. I'm ready, sir – I'll do it! If you could only just give me the chance to speak to him, even for a moment, to open my heart to him.

FATHER (*approaching the* SON, *threateningly*). You'll do it! You'll do it for your mother! For your mother, d'you hear?

SON (*more determined than ever*). I'm doing nothing!

FATHER (*seizing him by the lapels and shaking him*). For God's sake, do as you're told! Do it! Can't you hear what she's saying? What kind of son are you? Have you no feelings?

SON (*seizing him in turn*). No! No, I haven't! Let that be an end to it!

General uproar. The MOTHER, *terrified, tries to intervene and separate them.*

MOTHER. For God's sake, stop it! Stop it!

FATHER (*still holding onto him*). You'll do what you're told, you'll do it, d'you hear?

Grappling with him, the SON *finally throws the* FATHER *to the floor, near the staircase, to everyone's horror.*

SON. What in God's name's come over you, have you gone completely mad? Have you no self-respect, parading our disgrace in front of the whole world? Well, I'm having nothing to do with this, you can count me out. And that's entirely in line with our author's wishes – he didn't want us on stage!

DIRECTOR. But you've come here, haven't you?

SON (*pointing to the* FATHER). *His* idea, not mine!

DIRECTOR. But you're here as well.

SON. It was him – he was the one who wanted to come, dragging all of us along, and fixing up with you back there what to put in the play – not just things that really happened, as if that wasn't bad enough, but even things that didn't!

DIRECTOR. All right, tell me, then – at least you can tell me what *did* happen! You left the room without saying a word, right?

SON (*after a moment's hesitation*). Yes. Not a word. Deliberately, so as not to make a scene.

DIRECTOR (*urging him on*). Good, good, then what? What did you do next?

Anxiously watched by the others, the SON *takes a few steps across the stage.*

SON. Nothing . . . Walked through the garden . . . (*Breaks off, gloomy, deep in thought.*)

DIRECTOR (*urging him on again, clearly struck by his reticence*). Well? You were walking through the garden?

SON (*in despair, covering his face with his arm*). Why do you want me to talk about it, sir? It's horrible!

The MOTHER, *trembling all over, gives a muffled groan and looks towards the pond. The* DIRECTOR *observes her look, and turns to the* SON *with rising apprehension.*

DIRECTOR (*quietly*). The little girl?

SON (*staring straight ahead, into the auditorium*). There, in the pond.

FATHER (*still on the floor, pointing to the* MOTHER, *pityingly*). And she was following him, sir.

DIRECTOR (*to the* SON, *anxiously*). And then you . . . ?

SON (*slowly, still staring straight ahead*). I ran. I rushed up to pull her out . . . Then all of a sudden I stopped – there was something behind those trees and it made my blood run cold. It was the boy, that boy standing there motionless, with a crazed look in his eyes, staring at his little sister, lying drowned in the pond.

The STEPDAUGHTER, *still bent over the pond, concealing the* LITTLE GIRL, *responds like an echo from the deep, sobbing desperately. A pause.*

I started to move towards him, and then . . .

He goes back behind the trees where the YOUNG BOY *remains hidden, and a revolver shot rings out. The* MOTHER *cries out in anguish, and runs up along with the* SON *and all the* ACTORS, *a confused melée.*

MOTHER. Oh, my son! My son! (*Then above the general cacophony.*) Help! Help!

Amid the uproar, the DIRECTOR *is trying to make his way through, while the* YOUNG BOY *is lifted up by the head and feet and carried off behind the white backcloth.*

90 SIX CHARACTERS IN SEARCH OF AN AUTHOR

DIRECTOR. Is he wounded? Is he really wounded?

With the exception of the DIRECTOR *and the* FATHER, *who is still on the floor by the staircase, everyone else disappears behind the sky-cloth, where they remain for a while anxiously murmuring. Eventually, the* ACTORS *re-enter onto the stage, from both sides of the backdrop.*

LEADING LADY (*re-entering from the right, very upset*). He's dead! The poor boy! He's dead! Oh, this is terrible!

LEADING MAN (*re-entering from the left, laughing*). What d'you mean, dead? He's just pretending! He's acting! Don't believe it.

OTHER ACTORS (*from the right*). Pretending? No! This is real, it's real – he's dead!

OTHER ACTORS (*from the left*). No, no – it's all an act! Make-believe!

FATHER (*standing up and shouting over them*). There's no make-believe! This is real, sirs – reality! Reality! (*In despair, he also disappears behind the backcloth.*)

DIRECTOR (*at the end of his tether*). Make-believe! Reality! Oh, the hell with the lot of you! Lights! Lights! Lights!

Suddenly the whole stage and auditorium are flooded with an extremely bright light. The DIRECTOR *breathes a sigh of relief as if awakened from a nightmare, and they all look at one another, bewildered and disorientated.*

God, I've never known anything like it! This has cost us a whole day, you know. (*Looks at his watch.*) Go on, off you go. There's nothing we can do here now. It's too late to re-start the rehearsal. I'll see you all this evening. (*And as*

soon as the ACTORS *have said their goodbyes.*) Right,
electrician – switch everything off!

*He no sooner says this, than the whole theatre is momentarily
plunged into darkness.*

Oh, for God's sake – leave me some light to see my feet!

*Instantly, behind the backdrop, as if caused by a faulty connection,
a green spotlight is switched on, projecting large-scale silhouettes of
the* CHARACTERS, *with the exception of the* YOUNG BOY
and the LITTLE GIRL. *Seeing these, the* DIRECTOR *leaps
down from the stage, terrified. Simultaneously, the spotlight behind
the backdrop goes out, and the stage is restored to blue nocturnal
light as before. Slowly, from behind the right-hand side of the
backcloth, the* SON *is first to emerge, followed by the* MOTHER,
her arms outstretched towards him; then the FATHER *appears
from the left-hand side. They come to a halt in centre stage, and
remain there motionless, as if in a trance. Last to emerge, from the
left, is the* STEPDAUGHTER, *who runs towards one of the
staircases. She pauses briefly on the first step to look round at the
other three, then bursts into shrill laughter, before rushing headlong
down into the auditorium and up the central aisle between the seats;
once more she stops and laughs, looking back at the three remaining
on stage. Finally, she disappears from the auditorium, but her
laughter can still be heard from the foyer. After a few moments,
the curtain falls.*